23 Ready-To-Go Lesson Plans
SOCIAL STUDIES
GRADE 3

www.themailbox.com

What Are Lifesaver Lessons®?

Lifesaver Lessons® are well-planned, easy-to-implement, curriculum-based lessons. Each lesson contains a complete materials list, step-by-step instructions, a reproducible activity or pattern, and several extension activities.

How Do I Use A Lifesaver Lessons® Unit?

Each Lifesaver Lesson is designed to decrease your preparation time and increase the amount of quality teaching time with your students. These lessons are great for introducing or reinforcing new concepts. Use the handy list below to see what types of materials to gather. After completing a lesson, be sure to check out the fun-filled extension activities.

What Materials Will I Need?

Most of the materials for each lesson can be easily found in your classroom or school. Check the list of materials below for any items you may need to gather or purchase.

- crayons
- markers
- chalk
- scissors
- glue
- tape
- centimeter rulers
- writing paper
- chart paper
- duplicating paper
- construction paper
- index cards
- stapler
- brads
- products with safety labels
- small box
- large United States map
- large world map
- globe
- rubber ball or beanbag

Project Editor:
Mary Lester

Writers:
Amy Erickson, Kimberly Fields, Ellen Fortson,
Heather Graley, Cynthia Holcomb, Nicole Iacovazzi,
Linda Manwiller, Geoffrey Mihalenko,
Stacie Stone Smith, Stephanie Smith,
Valerie Wood Smith, Laura Wagner

Artists:
Cathy Spangler Bruce, Pam Crane, Nick Greenwood,
Clevell Harris, Theresa Lewis, Rob Mayworth,
Kimberly Richard, Rebecca Saunders,
Barry Slate, Donna K. Teal

Cover Artist:
Kimberly Richard

Table Of Contents

Targeting Communities

Strengthen your sharpshooters' understanding of community settings with this motivating lesson!

Skill: Identifying urban, suburban, and rural settings

Estimated Lesson Time: 30 minutes

Teacher Preparation:
1. Duplicate page 5 for each student.
2. Draw a large target on the chalkboard. Starting from the center, label each section from the center out "urban," "suburban," and "rural" (see the illustration below).

Materials:
1 copy of page 5 for each student
scissors
glue
crayons

Background Information:
   There are three major community settings. An *urban* setting is in the city. A *suburban* setting has to do with a community that is just outside of or close to a city. A *rural* setting has to do with the country.
   Although each of the community settings have features in common, such as homes, they also have differences. For example, a skyscraper might be found in the city but probably not in the country.

Introducing The Lesson:

Ask students to think about the area in which they live. Encourage students to discuss the characteristics of their community, such as parks, schools, and trees. Next ask students if everyone lives in the same type of community as they do. Confirm that people live in different types of communities; then share the Background Information on page 3.

Steps:

1. Direct students' attention to the target on the chalkboard. Tell students to name characteristics that describe an urban setting. Write their responses in the corresponding section of the target (see the example below). Repeat this step for suburban and rural.

2. Distribute a copy of page 5 to each student. Review the directions with students and have each child complete the page independently.

3. Challenge students to complete the Bonus Box activity.

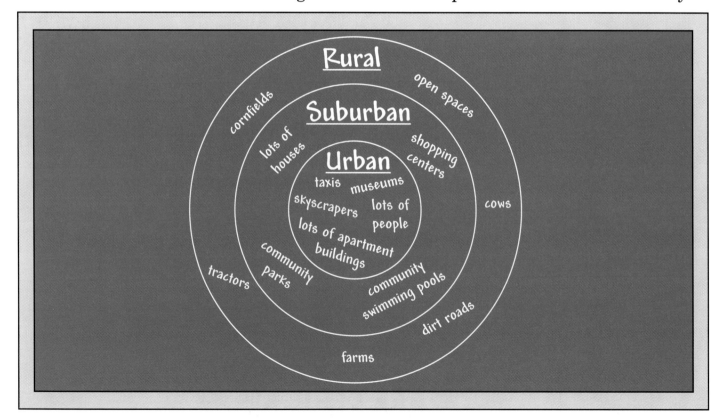

Identifying urban, suburban, and rural settings

Name _____

Targeting Communities

Write a definition for each community setting. Then read each card at the bottom of the page.
Decide which cards best fit in each community. Next color and cut out each card. Glue each card on its matching tree.

Rural

Definition:

Suburban

Definition:

Urban

Definition:

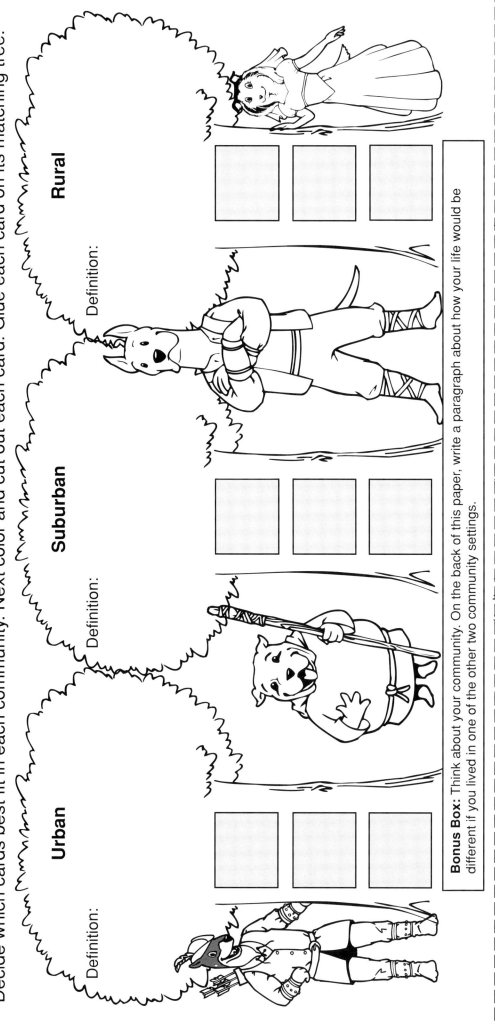

Bonus Box: Think about your community. On the back of this paper, write a paragraph about how your life would be different if you lived in one of the other two community settings.

community parks	museums	cows	tractors	houses	cornfields	skyscrapers	community swimming pools	taxis

5

COMMUNITIES

How To Extend The Lesson:

- Youngsters take aim at community settings with this center idea. First make a set of flash cards. On the front of each card, write a characteristic of one of the three community settings. On the back, write the setting to which the characteristic belongs. Then make a large target, labeling each section with a point value. Place the flash cards, the target, a beanbag, a supply of paper, and a pencil at the center. To complete the activity, a student places the target on the floor. Then he reads the front of a flash card, decides what the setting is, and checks his answer. If he is correct, he tosses the beanbag on the target and writes down the number of points he earned. If he is incorrect, he places the card in a discard pile and reviews it at the end of the game. He continues in this manner until all cards have been reviewed; then he totals his points and tries to beat that score the next time he plays.

- Showcase a collection of student work with this bulletin board idea. Give each student a white paper plate and a copy of the pattern below. In the center of the paper plate, instruct the student to color a picture of one of the three community settings. Then have her color the outer ridge of the plate red. On the arrow, direct her to write three descriptive sentences about the setting she drew. Then have her cut out the arrow, flip it over, and write the setting near the tip. Mount each paper plate and arrow (as shown) on a bulletin board titled "Hit The Bull's-Eye!" Encourage students to read the descriptions and then lift the tip of the arrow to check their guesses.

Pattern

Guess Which Community I Am!

1. _____

2. _____

3. _____

6 *Identifying urban, suburban, and rural settings*

Helping Hands

Help students learn that everyone wins when community members work together!

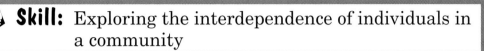

Skill: Exploring the interdependence of individuals in a community

Estimated Lesson Time: 45 minutes

Teacher Preparation:
1. Duplicate page 9 for each student.
2. Using a 12" x 18" sheet of construction paper, scissors, and markers, make a class puzzle. To do this, draw a desired picture or design that fills the page. Then cut it into puzzle pieces so that there is one piece for each student.

Materials:
1 copy of page 9 for each student
construction paper
markers
tape
scissors

Background Information:
A *community* is a place where people live and help each other. People in a community help one another by giving money to those in need and by sharing work. For example, doctors, nurses, technicians, and paramedics work together to help people become well. Depending upon one another is called *interdependence*.

Introducing The Lesson:

Give each student a puzzle piece. Explain to students that they will help each other solve a puzzle. In turn, have each student bring her piece to the chalkboard. Encourage the class to work together to determine where the pieces fit and then lightly tape them into place. When the puzzle is completed, acknowledge how the group worked together to finish the task.

Steps:

1. Explain to the class that they will be learning how people in a community work together to help one another. Share the Background Information on page 7.

2. Write the word *firefighter* on the chalkboard. Then ask students how firefighters help the community and list their responses under the word *firefighter*.

3. Repeat Step 2 using the words *police officer* and *emergency medical technician (EMT)*.

4. Distribute a copy of page 9 to each student. Encourage a class discussion about the illustration at the top of page 9. Guide students to understand the role of each person, such as the police officer directs traffic and keeps people out of harm's way. Then have each student complete the page independently.

5. Challenge students to complete the Bonus Box activity.

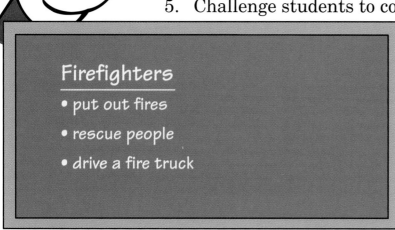

Firefighters
- put out fires
- rescue people
- drive a fire truck

Exploring the interdependence of individuals in a community

Helping Hands

Read each question below.
Use the picture above to answer each question.

1. How does the police officer help the citizens? _____

    _____

2. How does the police officer help the firefighters? _____

    _____

3. How do the EMTs help the firefighters? _____

    _____

4. How does the police officer help the EMTs? _____

    _____

5. How do the firefighters help the EMTs? _____

    _____

> **Bonus Box:** On the back of this paper, write one way the citizens in the picture can help either the firefighters, the police officer, or the EMTs.

How To Extend The Lesson:

- Have students give gifts to their community. On an index card, have each student write one way people in his community could help one another. Then instruct the student to glue his index card to a slightly larger piece of wrapping paper and add a bow. Mount the gifts on a bulletin board entitled "Presents To Our Community!"

- Explain to students that lending a hand at home can be a way of helping the community. Then read *The Berenstain Bears Lend A Helping Hand* by Jan and Stan Berenstain (Random House, Inc.; 1998) to your class. Encourage discussion about how the yard sale provided an opportunity for the cubs and Miz McGrizz to help one another. Next have each student trace her hand on a sheet of construction paper and cut it out. Then, on each finger, have her write a way she helps at home. In the palm, have each student draw a picture of helping at home and write "[Student's Name] Helps Out!" Next use the handprints to make a bulletin-board border or display them on a wall.

- Encourage students to help their community. Choose a day for students to pick up trash from the school grounds or contribute canned goods to needy families. Then reward your community helpers with a copy of the ribbon pattern shown.

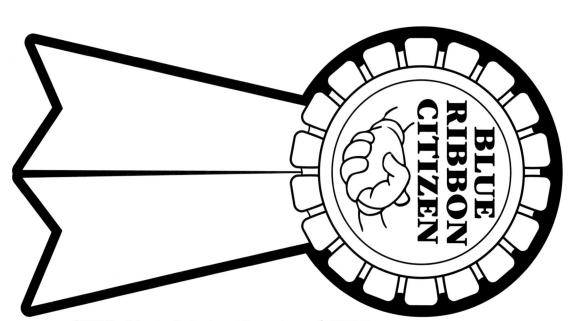

Exploring the interdependence of individuals in a community

Resource Roundup

Saddle up and get set to teach how natural resources affect community life with this rootin'-tootin' lesson!

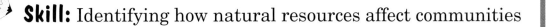

Skill: Identifying how natural resources affect communities

Estimated Lesson Time: 40 minutes

Teacher Preparation:
Duplicate page 13 for each student.

Materials:
1 copy of page 13 for each student

Background Information:
Natural resources are things found in nature that people can use. Natural resources are not made by people. Land, minerals, water, plants, animals, and climate are all natural resources. People use natural resources to make goods, such as food, fuel, and raw materials. Natural resources affect the types of recreation and jobs found in a community.

Introducing The Lesson:

Explain to students that *climate* is the average weather of a place over a period of years. Ask students to describe your community's climate. Record their responses on the chalkboard.

Steps:

1. Share with students the Background Information on page 11. Then ask them to describe how your community is affected by its climate.

2. Have students share examples of other natural resources in your community, such as a river or an ocean. Then ask them to describe how these resources affect the types of recreation (swimming) and jobs (lifeguarding) in your community.

3. Have students brainstorm a list of natural resources found in other communities that are different from theirs (see the list below for suggestions). Write students' ideas on the chalkboard. Challenge them to think of how each resource might affect a community.

4. Distribute a copy of page 13 to each student. Have a volunteer read aloud the directions at the top of the page. Have each child complete the reproducible independently.

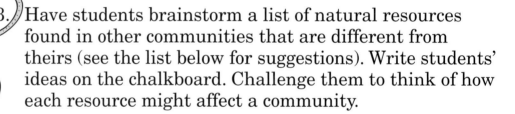

Resources In Other Communities

oil	cacti
warm climate	tropical birds
beaches	rainfall
snow	gold
canyons	seafood

Identifying how natural resources affect communities

Resource Roundup

Read each community's description.
Then read each clue.
Write an "I" next to each clue that describes Iceville.
Write an "S" next to each clue that describes Sunland.

Iceville

Iceville is a community located just below the North Pole. Its growing season is very short. Iceville has a large supply of oil beneath its icy ground. Iceville is located near a large frozen lake. There are also rich mineral deposits in this area.

Sunland

Sunland is a community that has a very warm climate. Sunland has lots of beaches and is a popular vacation spot. The waters near Sunland are full of tuna and other sea life. Sunland's growing season is very long.

	1. This area's beaches attract many tourists.		6. A large tuna-packing factory in this area provides many jobs.
	2. A big oil refinery is located in this community.		7. Many people work for the local mining company.
	3. Many biologists who study sea life work here.		8. There are many services provided for tourists in this community.
	4. Farming is an important industry in this area.		9. This community doesn't grow very many crops.
	5. Ice fishing is a form of recreation in this area.		10. During the winter, few people visit this community because of the cold climate.

How To Extend The Lesson:

• This hands-on activity focuses on the natural resources in your community. From discarded magazines, have each child cut out pictures representing natural resources found in your community. Direct him to glue his cutouts on a sheet of construction paper in an overlapping fashion to create a collage. Post the completed projects on a bulletin board titled "Rounding Up Our Natural Resources."

• Divide your class into small groups. Give each group a section of employment ads from your local newspaper. Then have the group cut out three job ads that are based on the natural resources in your community. (These might include an ad for a coal miner, a lifeguard, an oil refinery worker, or a commercial fisherman.) When the allotted time is over, ask each group to name the jobs they found and tell how they relate to your community's natural resources. Discuss with students how the types of jobs might change if your community had different natural resources.

• Have students create brochures featuring the natural resources in your community. With students, brainstorm and write on the chalkboard a list of your community's natural resources. To create a brochure, a student folds a 9" x 12" sheet of white construction paper in thirds. She then unfolds the paper and writes the title "[Community's name]'s Natural Resources" on the back of the first section. Then she personalizes the resulting cover as desired. On each of the five remaining brochure pages, the student writes a sentence about a different resource from the list on the board and illustrates it. After students share their brochures, display the completed projects in your school's media center.

Gators Guard Community Rights

Teach students about community law with this snappy activity!

Skill: Identifying the need for and the use of community laws

Estimated Lesson Time: 45 minutes

Teacher Preparation:
1. Duplicate page 17 for each student.
2. Obtain three or four products with safety labels or cautions, such as a bottle of correction fluid, the package of a toy, and a bottle of glue.

Materials:
1 copy of page 17
3 or 4 products with safety labels or cautions
scissors
glue

Background Information:
Community laws help people live together in a fair way. City leaders decide on laws that will benefit the community and protect the people. Not all communities have the same laws.

Some laws protect the health and safety of people. For example, a law that requires a person to ride his or her bike on the road rather than on the sidewalk protects pedestrians.

Other laws are made to keep order and protect property. For example, dogs that are allowed to roam neighborhoods can destroy property by turning over trash cans and digging in yards. A law that keeps dogs from roaming protects people's property.

Communities are responsible for enforcing the laws. Police officers, judges, and other officials make sure that laws are followed and people who violate them are punished.

Introducing The Lesson:

Display the products that contain safety labels. Ask students why some products come with a safety label. Guide students in understanding that labels protect people by advising them of possible dangers.

Steps:

1. Tell students that, like safety labels on products, community laws help protect people and keep them safe. Next share the Background Information on page 15 with youngsters. Ask students to tell about community laws with which they are familiar. Then lead students in a discussion about why each law listed below is needed. Write their responses on the chalkboard.
   - Do not let your dog roam the community.
   - Remove all poison ivy and poison oak from your yard.
   - Ride your bicycle on the right-hand side of the road.
   - Bag yard clippings rather than burning them.
   - Do not have open barrels or containers in your yard. *(Mosquitoes cause health problems when they breed in the rainwater that collects.)*

2. Distribute a copy of page 17 to each student. Ask a student volunteer to read **Gators Guard Community Rights** and the directions on page 17 aloud. Then instruct each student to fill in the blanks independently, color the pattern, and cut it out. Next, have the student fold the pattern on the thin line and glue the back of the two halves together. If desired, punch a hole at the top of each project and tie a length of yarn through the hole. Use tape to suspend the projects from each student's desk.

Identifying the need for and the use of community laws

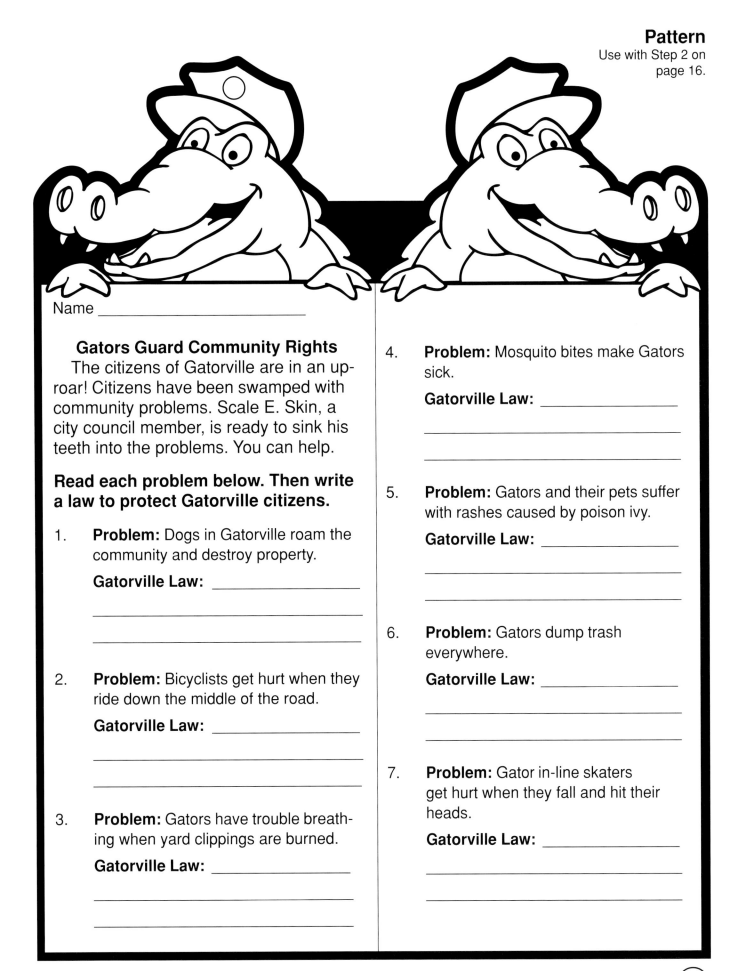

Name _____

Gators Guard Community Rights

The citizens of Gatorville are in an up-roar! Citizens have been swamped with community problems. Scale E. Skin, a city council member, is ready to sink his teeth into the problems. You can help.

Read each problem below. Then write a law to protect Gatorville citizens.

1. **Problem:** Dogs in Gatorville roam the community and destroy property.

    Gatorville Law: _____

    _____

    _____

2. **Problem:** Bicyclists get hurt when they ride down the middle of the road.

    Gatorville Law: _____

    _____

    _____

3. **Problem:** Gators have trouble breath-ing when yard clippings are burned.

    Gatorville Law: _____

    _____

    _____

4. **Problem:** Mosquito bites make Gators sick.

    Gatorville Law: _____

    _____

    _____

5. **Problem:** Gators and their pets suffer with rashes caused by poison ivy.

    Gatorville Law: _____

    _____

    _____

6. **Problem:** Gators dump trash everywhere.

    Gatorville Law: _____

    _____

    _____

7. **Problem:** Gator in-line skaters get hurt when they fall and hit their heads.

    Gatorville Law: _____

    _____

    _____

How To Extend The Lesson:

- Organize students into small groups and have them role-play city leaders considering a proposed law. Write several proposals on the chalkboard, such as "Should adults be required to supervise their children at public parks?" or "Should people with in-line skates be required to pass a safety test before using them in public places?" Instruct each group to select a proposal to discuss. After an appropriate amount of time, have each group report its recommendations to the class.

- Instruct each student to think of a law—serious or funny—to propose to city leaders. Examples of some laws may include that children must not play outside after dark or that all children must eat candy every day. Then have each child write a letter explaining why she thinks her proposal should become law. Allow time for each student volunteer to read her letter aloud and hold a class discussion on the pros and cons of her proposition.

- Invite a city leader, such as a city council member, to visit your classroom. Ask him or her to discuss how laws are made in your community, which laws have been made most recently, and which ones have become outdated due to changes in the community. Encourage students to ask your guest to explain any laws that they don't fully understand.

Why do we have a city ordinance that does not permit a household to hold more than two yard sales a year?

Identifying the need for and the use of community laws

Count On Your Community

Teach youngsters that rights and responsibilities go hand in hand to create a top-notch community.

Skill: Identifying rights and responsibilities of a good citizen

Estimated Lesson Time: 40 minutes

Teacher Preparation:
Duplicate page 21 for each student.

Materials:
1 copy of page 21 for each student
scissors
glue

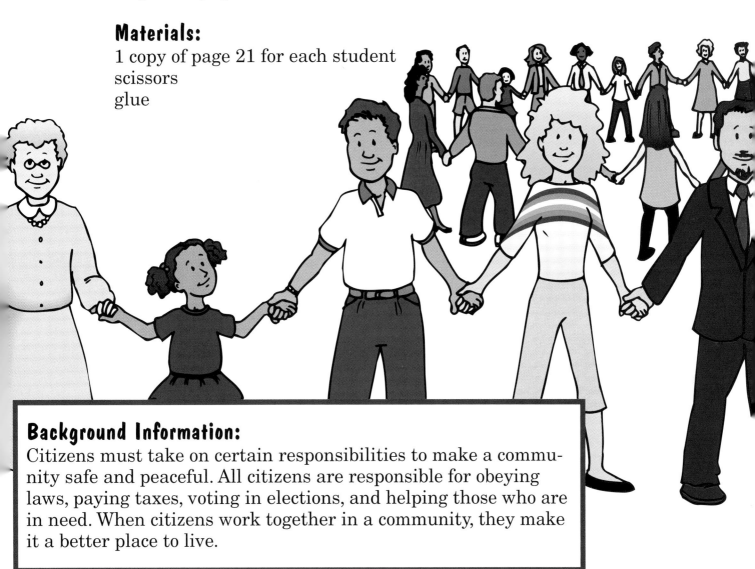

Background Information:
Citizens must take on certain responsibilities to make a community safe and peaceful. All citizens are responsible for obeying laws, paying taxes, voting in elections, and helping those who are in need. When citizens work together in a community, they make it a better place to live.

Introducing The Lesson:

Have students name workers they see in school, such as teachers and cafeteria workers. Record their responses on the chalkboard. Next ask students what might happen if these workers did not do their work.

Steps:

1. Encourage students to discuss the ways these people work together each day. Reinforce that students have a right to an education and that everyone—school staff and students—must work together to have a successful school day.

2. Explain to students that people in a *community* also have certain rights and responsibilities. Share the Background Information on page 19 with students.

3. Write the words *rights* and *responsibilities* on the chalkboard. Under the word *rights,* list places such as parks, libraries, schools, and youth centers. Point out to students that all citizens have a right to enjoy these places. Ask students to name the responsibilities involved in having these places in a community (see the suggestions below). Record responses on the chalkboard.

4. Distribute scissors, glue, and a copy of page 21 to each student.

5. Ask a volunteer read the speech bubbles and the directions at the top of the page. Have students complete the page independently.

6. Challenge students to complete the Bonus Box.

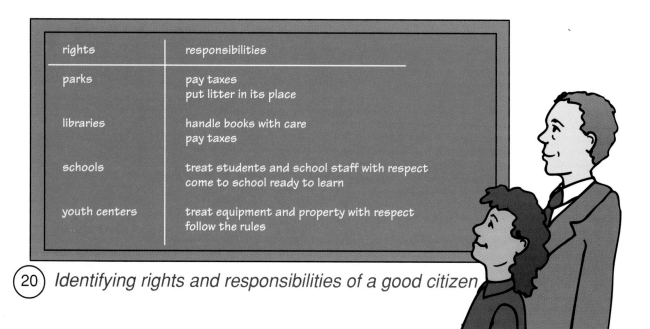

rights	responsibilities
parks	pay taxes put litter in its place
libraries	handle books with care pay taxes
schools	treat students and school staff with respect come to school ready to learn
youth centers	treat equipment and property with respect follow the rules

Identifying rights and responsibilities of a good citizen

Count On Your Community

Everyone in a community has certain rights and responsibilities.

It is your **responsibility** to keep your community safe and happy.

You have a **right** to enjoy a safe and happy place to live.

Read each sentence.
Cut out each sentence and glue it under the correct heading.

My Community Rights	My Community Responsibilities

Bonus Box: On the back of this paper, write five things you could do to be a responsible citizen.

I play at a neighborhood park.	I recycle materials.
I put litter in its correct place.	I can count on others if I need help.
I follow safety rules.	I check out books from the library.
I feel safe in my neighborhood.	I keep my dog from roaming the community.
I help others in need.	I live in a caring community.

21

How To Extend The Lesson:

- Share with students *Roxaboxen* by Alice McLerran (Puffin Books, 1992), the story of an imaginative community. Point out how the children in the story work together to build a community complete with a mayor and police officers. Ask students to identify the rights and responsibilities described in the story. Then extend the lesson by having small groups of students create imaginative communities of their own. Provide materials such as shoeboxes, clean milk cartons, construction paper, craft sticks, pebbles, scissors, and glue. If desired, have students fashion wooden clothespin people to populate their communities. Encourage each group to include the buildings and people needed to make the community a good place to live. Allow students time to share their completed projects with one another.

- Have students make posters encouraging citizens to act responsibly. Provide each student with crayons and a sheet of white construction paper. Instruct each child to focus on a responsibility that is of concern in her community. Display the completed projects in the hallway for everyone to see.

- Make a student-generated chart to show how community responsibilities are delegated. To do this, write the words *mayor, city council, judge, police officers, citizens,* and *visitors* on the left side of a large sheet of chart paper. Have students describe the responsibilities of each person while you record their responses on the chart (see the example below). Display the completed chart in the classroom for reference during your study of communities.

Our Community

mayor: leader of the city or town
city council: helps make community laws
judge: decides consequences for lawbreakers
police officers: help keep people safe
citizens: follow community rules and help others
visitors: follow rules of the community

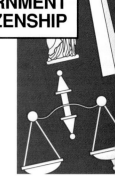

Put It To A Vote!

Guide your young voters through a mock election with this award-winning lesson!

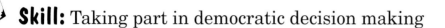

Skill: Taking part in democratic decision making

Estimated Lesson Time: 45 minutes

Teacher Preparation:

1. Duplicate page 25 for each student, plus two extras.
2. Color and cut out the two extra campaign ribbons and discard the ballots. Make sure each ribbon is colored differently.
3. Set up a private area for voting in the classroom.
4. Obtain a box or container to serve as a ballot box.

Materials:

1 copy of page 25 for each student
2 differently colored campaign ribbons
ballot box
scissors
crayons
tape

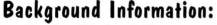

Background Information:

In the United States, every citizen has the right to vote. When it is time to choose new candidates or laws, an election is held. Many citizens go to places called *polls* to cast their votes.

In some elections, people mark a *ballot*—a sheet of paper used to cast a secret vote. A voter goes into a private voting booth and places a mark next to his choice on the ballot; then he places his ballot in the ballot box. In some cases, a voting machine is used instead of a paper ballot. After everyone has had a chance to vote, the votes are counted and the outcome is announced.

Introducing The Lesson:

Begin the lesson by taping the two colored ribbons to the chalkboard. Label one ribbon *A* and the other *B*. Inform the class that later in the lesson each student will vote for the ribbon of his choice.

Steps:

1. Explain that one of the most important parts of an election is the *campaign* that occurs beforehand. In a campaign, some people try to convince voters which way to vote. Instruct students to choose a ribbon and write a campaign slogan for it, such as "Green, red, and blue is the ribbon for you!" Have students read their slogans aloud; then encourage students to decide which ribbon they prefer.

2. Ask students to put their heads down for privacy. Have them raise their hands for choice A or B. Then tally the votes on the chalkboard. If there is a tie, add your vote to the results.

3. Have students look at the results. Explain that the choice with the most votes is the winner by *majority rule,* because more than half of the class voted for it. Share the Background Information on page 23 with students. Remove the ribbons from the chalkboard.

4. Inform students that they will vote for other colors to be used in new campaign ribbons. Distribute a copy of page 25 and a pair of scissors to each student. Then instruct each child to cut out his ballot. Have each student cast his vote by marking one box in each section; then have him place his ballot in the ballot box.

5. While students are voting, write the six categories and their choices on the chalkboard. Enlist students' help in tallying the votes. Have students color their ribbons according to the election results. Then have students cut out and wear their ribbons.

outer circle
orange ЖШ I
purple ЖШ IIII

wavy stripes
purple ЖШ ЖШ
orange ЖШ

inner circle
red ЖШ ЖШ I
blue IIII

stars
orange ЖШ I
yellow ЖШ IIII

letters
black ЖШ
white ЖШ ЖШ

ribbons
green ЖШ ЖШ II
purple III

Put It To A Vote!

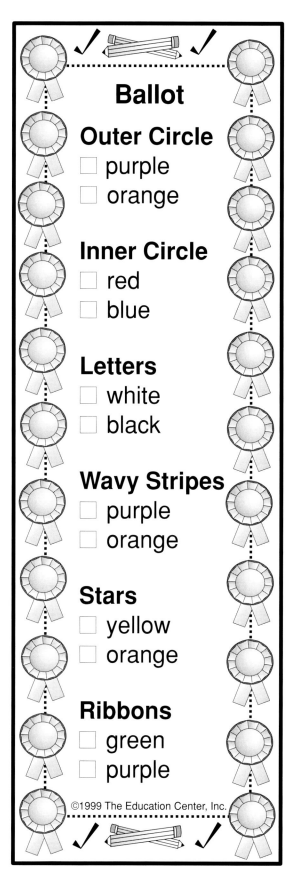

Ballot

Outer Circle
☐ purple
☐ orange

Inner Circle
☐ red
☐ blue

Letters
☐ white
☐ black

Wavy Stripes
☐ purple
☐ orange

Stars
☐ yellow
☐ orange

Ribbons
☐ green
☐ purple

©1999 The Education Center, Inc.

How To Extend The Lesson:

- Explain to students that voters must meet certain requirements in order to vote. A voter must be at least 18 years of age, a citizen of the United States, and registered to vote. A registered voter is given a voter registration card. Obtain a few real voter registration cards for students to examine; then have students make their own voter registration cards to be used for classroom voting.

- Organize students into small groups to create a class mascot. Have each group discuss what its mascot will look like and decide upon a name for it. Next, instruct each group to list five characteristics that would make its mascot a good choice, and then draw a picture of it. Have each group campaign for its mascot in front of another class. After each group has given its campaign speech, hold an election to vote for the new mascot. Allow both classes to vote and hear the results of the election. Display the pictures of all mascots in a prominent location in your classroom.

- Have each student write a list of three topics on which the class could vote, such as which book to be read aloud or which game to play during the next indoor recess. Collect the lists and choose one topic. Program one copy of the ballot below with the topic and the choices on which to vote. Then duplicate a class set of the ballot and have students vote. If desired, have each student show her voter registration card before voting (see the first idea on this page). Repeat the activity in a similar manner with other topics.

Ballot

Ballot

Topic _____

Choices _____

☐ ☐ ☐ ☐ ☐

VOTE!

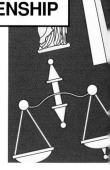

A Star-Spangled Tour

*Send students on a trip to see impressive U.S. monuments
and landforms—without leaving their seats!*

Skill: Identifying significant U.S. monuments and landforms

Estimated Lesson Time: 45 minutes

Teacher Preparation:
1. Duplicate page 29 for each student.
2. Program a set of index cards
   as shown below.

Materials:
1 copy of page 29 for each student
one 12" x 18" sheet of light-colored
   construction paper for each student
set of programmed index cards
large United States map
scissors
glue
crayons
tape

Background Information:
Many famous U.S. landforms are known for their natural beauty. The Grand Canyon is a spectacular gorge in Arizona and the Everglades are beautiful marshlands in southern Florida.

U.S. monuments honor our nation and remind us of the freedoms we enjoy. Mount Rushmore National Memorial is a huge sculpture in South Dakota that honors four U.S. presidents. The Statue of Liberty is a sculpture that towers above Liberty Island in New York and has become a symbol of freedom.

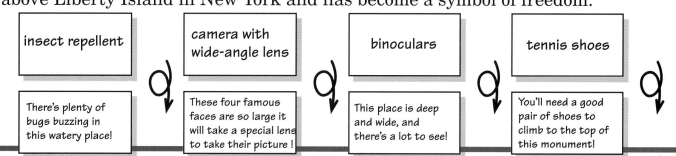

insect repellent	camera with wide-angle lens	binoculars	tennis shoes
There's plenty of bugs buzzing in this watery place!	These four famous faces are so large it will take a special lens to take their picture!	This place is deep and wide, and there's a lot to see!	You'll need a good pair of shoes to climb to the top of this monument!

Introducing The Lesson:

Tell students you are going to take them on a trip across the United States to visit famous monuments and landforms. Then draw a large outline of a suitcase on the chalkboard. Post the programmed index cards (item-side facing up) inside the suitcase. Next write the names of each monument or landform around the suitcase. Explain to students that they will need the items in the suitcase for an imaginary visit to important U.S. monuments and landforms.

Steps:

1. Remove the card with the word *binoculars* on it. Then read the back of the card aloud. Ask students to guess which U.S. landform they are visiting. Confirm that it is the Grand Canyon. Point to its location (Arizona) on the United States map.

2. Repeat the procedure as you remove each card from the suitcase, locating Mount Rushmore in South Dakota, the Statue of Liberty in New York, and the Everglades in Florida.

3. Tell students that now that the trip has been completed, each child will create a photo album page featuring these U.S. monuments and landforms.

4. Distribute a 12" x 18" sheet of light-colored construction paper, scissors, crayons, glue, and a copy of page 29 to each student.

5. To create a photo album page, a student colors and cuts out the patterns on page 29. Next he turns his construction paper lengthwise and glues each monument or landform picture along the top. Next the student glues two matching information strips under each picture. Then, below the information strips, he writes a paragraph about his imaginary visit to each monument and landform. When students have completed their projects, compile the pages into a class photo album. Add a construction paper cover titled "We've Seen The Sights!" and place the album in the clasroom library for students to enjoy.

Mount Rushmore

Grand Canyon

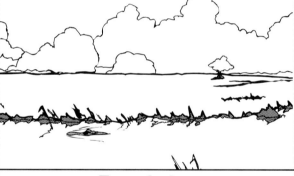

Everglades

Statue of Liberty

These marshlands, found in Florida, have plains of grass and trees.

It's a long way to the top! From its feet to the tip of its torch, this sculpture is over 150 feet high.

Carved by the Colorado River, this hole in the ground is over one mile deep in places.

You'll find a variety of wildlife here including alligators, cougars, manatees, and many birds.

This huge sculpture of four U.S. presidents is found in the Black Hills of South Dakota.

What a popular place! Each year about two million people visit this statue of a robed woman.

These four faces are George Washington, Thomas Jefferson, Theodore Roosevelt, and Abraham Lincoln.

At sunset the red and brown layers in this canyon's walls are a beautiful sight.

How To Extend The Lesson:

- Have each student select and research a famous U.S. land-form or monument. Assign or, if desired, have each student select a landform or monument (refer to the list below). Provide references, such as encyclopedias and books, for the student to use to research her topic. Next, on a large sheet of construction paper, have the student draw an illustration of her landform or monument and list several interesting facts about it, including its location. Display the completed posters in the hallway as a tribute to our country's national treasures.

  Niagara Falls
  Yellowstone National Park
  Washington Monument
  Lincoln Memorial
  Carlsbad Caverns National Park

  Pikes Peak
  Great Salt Lake
  Mojave Desert
  The Gateway Arch
  Vietnam Veterans Memorial

- Tap into your students' creativity by turning your classroom into a souvenir shop. Supply students with construction paper, markers, sequins, yarn, glue, and other art materials. Then assign each pair of students a different famous American landform or monument. Instruct students to create souvenirs—such as postcards, bumper stickers, pennants, jewelry, posters, and maps—to represent their assigned topics. When students have finished the assignment, have each pair present its completed inventory to the class, describing each souvenir. Then keep the items on display throughout your study of landforms and monuments.

- Play "American Places Pursuit" as a class guessing game. Give each child an index card. Have her select a famous landform or monument that has been studied in class, then follow the samples shown to write a "What Am I?" riddle about it. Have her write the answer at the bottom of the card. Next collect the cards and place them in a container. Then divide the class into two teams. In turn, one member from each team takes a card and reads it to the other team. Award a point for each correct answer.

My mountain has the tallest peak in the U.S. What am I?

Mount McKinley

I am an amazing waterfall. What am I?

Niagra Falls

I am a statue of our 16th president. What am I?

Lincoln Memorial

Letter-Perfect Leaders

When it comes to learning about leaders, this first-class lesson really delivers!

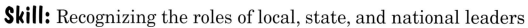

Skill: Recognizing the roles of local, state, and national leaders

Estimated Lesson Time: 30 minutes

Teacher Preparation:
1. Draw three large, concentric circles on the chalkboard.
2. Duplicate page 33 for each student.

Materials:
1 copy of page 33 per student
scissors
glue

Background Information:
Government in the United States has three levels—local, state, and national. Each level has a leader who works to meet the needs and wants of the people in his community: the citizens. The local, state, and national leaders are the mayor, governor, and president of the United States, respectively. Each leader's role in the community is described below.

• Mayor
—Works in city hall
—Helps establish city laws and make sure that they are followed
—Manages the libraries and the police, fire, transportation, and sanitation departments at the local level

• Governor
—Works in the state capitol
—Helps establish state laws and make sure that they are followed
—Manages education, public safety, recreation, welfare, and conservation at the state level

• President of the United States
—Works in the White House in Washington, DC
—Helps establish federal laws and make sure that they are followed
—Acts as the Commander in Chief of the Army, Navy, Air Force, and Marines
—Determines U.S. relations with other nations

Introducing The Lesson:

Direct students' attention to the circles on the board. Explain that the circles represent three communities to which each of them belong. Write "Local" in the smallest circle. Tell youngsters that their town or city is the local community. Ask youngsters to identify a larger community of which their town or city is part. Verify that their town or city is part of the state community; then write "State" on the next larger circle. Lead youngsters to name the community to which the state belongs—the nation—and write "National" on the largest circle. Tell students that they will learn about the job of each community's leader.

Steps:

1. Beginning with the local community, use the Background Information on page 31 to identify the leader of each community represented on the chalkboard and to describe his role.

2. Ask youngsters to identify similarities and differences among the roles of the three leaders discussed.

3. Tell students that it is important for citizens to let their leaders know how they feel about community issues. Name several topics that affect communities, such as building a new city library, protecting a state park, or establishing a national school curriculum. Ask students to identify the leader with whom it would be most appropriate to discuss each topic.

4. Explain that many citizens share their opinions and ideas with community leaders by writing letters to them. Tell youngsters that for this activity, they will imagine they are writing letters to a mayor, a governor, and the president. Give each student a copy of page 33, a pair of scissors, and glue. Have him cut out the envelopes on the dotted lines, then follow the directions on his sheet.

5. Challenge students to complete the Bonus Box activity.

Name _____

Letter-Perfect Leaders

For each topic, decide who would be the best community leader to write.
Glue an envelope beside each topic to show your answer.

1. building a bigger and better city library

2. an idea for a new national song

3. cutting down a forest so that the state highway can be made bigger

4. a state law that would make the school year longer

5. adding a baseball diamond to the city park

6. City Council's plan to outlaw bike riding after 4:00 P.M.

7. making a new holiday called National Bubble Gum Day

8. changing the state license plate design

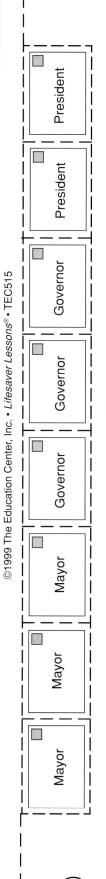

Bonus Box: On the back of this sheet, list three things you would do if you were the governor.

©1999 The Education Center, Inc. • *Lifesaver Lessons®* • TEC515

President

President

Governor

Governor

Governor

Mayor

Mayor

Mayor

33

How To Extend The Lesson:

- Use this bulletin-board idea to extend students' learning about leaders. Tack two lengths of yarn on the board to visually divide it into three equal-size columns. Mount cards labeled "Local," "State," and "National" at the top of the columns. On each of several days, provide students with newspapers. Have students cut out articles about issues at each of these levels. Mount articles related to the mayor's, governor's, and president's roles on red, white, and blue paper, respectively. Staple them onto the board in the appropriate columns. After an article is added to the display, read it aloud and discuss the issue featured.

- This class activity is perfect for reviewing the jobs of government leaders! On each of several slips of paper, write a different clue about the job of a mayor, governor, or the president. For example, write "works in the state capitol" as a clue for governor. Fold each slip and place it in a container. Give each student three index cards. Have him label his cards "Mayor," "Governor," and "President." To begin, take a strip from the container and read it aloud. Ask each student to identify which leader the clue describes by holding up his corresponding card. Look at the raised cards to check students' accuracy. Ask a youngster who is holding the correct card to name the leader. Continue with a desired number of additional clues in a like manner.

- Reinforce students' understanding of local, state, and national leaders' jobs with this step booklet project. To make his booklet, each youngster needs a 7" x 10" piece of red construction paper, a 9" x 12" piece of white construction paper, and a 12" x 15" piece of blue construction paper. He folds each paper in half; then staples the white and red papers atop the blue paper as shown. The youngster labels the red paper "Mayor," the white paper "Governor," and the blue paper "President." Next he describes each leader's job on a separate piece of writing paper sized to fit the corresponding page of his booklet. Finally, the student glues each description onto the appropriate page. Invite each youngster to share his work, and then tell which of the three jobs he would most like to have and why.

Ready, Set, Race!

Students will "purr-fect" their understanding of cardinal and intermediate directions with these two cool cats!

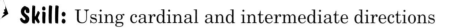

Skill: Using cardinal and intermediate directions

Estimated Lesson Time: 40 minutes

Teacher Preparation:
1. Duplicate page 37 for each student.
2. Label each wall or corner in your classroom with the appropriate cardinal or intermediate direction.
3. Draw a grid (like the one shown on page 36) on the chalkboard.

Materials:
1 copy of page 37 for each student
8 labeled signs

Background Information:
The four *cardinal directions* are north, south, east, and west. These directions are represented by the letters *N, E, S,* and *W* on a *compass rose*. A compass rose indicates directions on a map.

Intermediate directions are located halfway between the cardinal directions on a compass rose. The intermediate directions are northeast (NE), southeast (SE), southwest (SW), and northwest (NW).

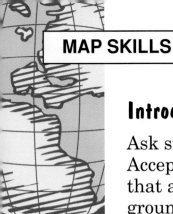

Introducing The Lesson:

Ask students what type of activities might require the use of a compass. Accept responses such as hiking or sailing. Then explain to students that a map has a compass called a compass rose. Next share the Background Information on page 35 with students. Then draw a simple compass rose on the chalkboard and label the cardinal and intermediate directions.

Steps:

1. Refer students to the cardinal and intermediate directions on the classroom walls. Direct students to stand, face the north wall, and quietly march in place. Announce a direction and have students turn and face that direction while marching in place. Call out another direction, giving students time to change directions. Continue in this same manner until students demonstrate an understanding of cardinal and intermediate directions. Then ask students to return to their seats.

2. Draw a flower in one of the boxes of the grid, and a star in another box. Announce a direction, such as "Go north two boxes." Instruct a student volunteer to start at the flower and draw a chalk line according to your oral directions. When the student has completed the first step, have other students follow similar oral directions until the line reaches the star. Then erase the flower, star, and line. Redraw the star and flower in different boxes. Repeat the process until students have a good understanding of using directions on a grid.

3. Distribute a copy of page 37 to each student. Review the directions with students and have each child complete the page independently.

4. Challenge students to complete the Bonus Box activity.

Ready, Set, Race!

Read the clues below the grid.
Draw the paths Casey and Smitty take to the stuffed mouse.
Then answer the question below.

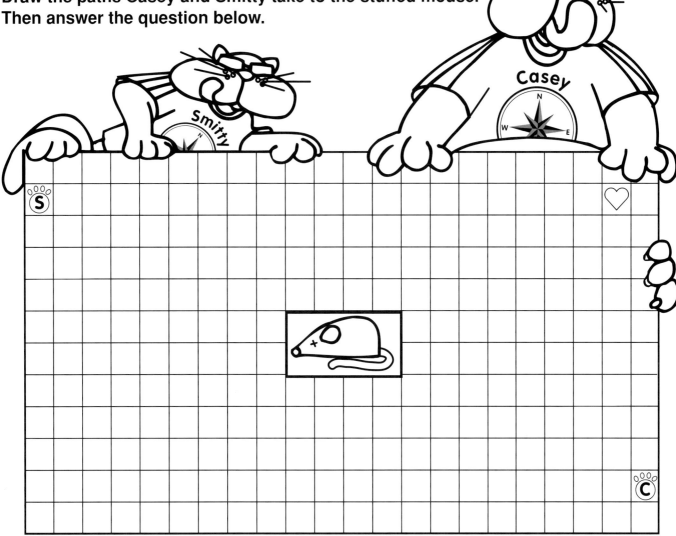

Begin at the pawprint marked (S) for Smitty .
1. Go south 2 blocks.
2. Go southeast 3 blocks.
3. Go southwest 1 block.
4. Go south 3 blocks.
5. Go northeast 2 blocks.
6. Go east 4 blocks.

Begin at the pawprint marked (C) for Casey.
1. Go north 2 blocks.
2. Go northwest 2 blocks.
3. Go west 2 blocks.
4. Go northwest 3 blocks.
5. Go west 2 blocks.
6. Go south 2 blocks.

Which cat got to the stuffed mouse? _____

Bonus Box: Draw a path for a third cat. Start the cat's path at the heart in the upper right-hand corner of the grid. Change directions at least three times. Finish the path at the stuffed mouse. On another sheet of paper, write the directions of the path.

How To Extend The Lesson:

- Students demonstrate their understanding of cardinal and intermediate directions with this engaging game. Have eight students stand in a circle, facing center. Tell the class to imagine the eight children are standing on a compass rose. Review the cardinal or intermediate direction that each of the eight children represents. Next ask a seated child to stand in the center of the circle and face north. Then ask the child in the center a question, such as "Who is standing northwest of you?" If the response is correct, the northwest student confirms it. Then the child in the center chooses a seated student to take his place. If the response is incorrect, the child in the center and the northwest student trade places. Continue in this manner until all students have had a chance to participate in some aspect of the game.

- When students are out of the classroom, hide a small object such as a stuffed mouse or a chalkboard eraser. Guide a student volunteer to the item by giving her a series of directional clues, such as "Take five giant steps northwest." Continue giving clues until she has found the item. Have another student volunteer cover his eyes as you hide the item in a different location. Have the student uncover his eyes and play the game again.

- Duplicate page 37 and cut out the grid. Then duplicate a copy of the grid for each student. Instruct the student to write a set of directional clues for Casey and Smitty, changing directions at least four times. After all students have completed the assignment, have them exchange papers and mark the paths according to the directions. Then have each student return his paper to its original owner to be checked.

Begin at the S pawprint.
1. Go east 6 blocks.
2. Go south 8 blocks
3. Go east 9 blocks
4. Go north west 3 blocks.

Blasting Off With Grids

Launch your study of grids with this far-reaching unit!

Skill: Using a grid

Estimated Lesson Time: 45 minutes

Teacher Preparation:

1. Duplicate page 41 for each student.
2. Label each of six sheets of construction paper with one of the following letters or numerals: *A, B, C, 1, 2,* and *3* (one letter or numeral per sheet).
3. Using masking tape, create a 3 x 3 grid on the classroom floor. Each box needs to be large enough for a person to stand in.

Materials:

1 copy of page 41 for each student
masking tape
6 sheets of construction paper
marker

I'm at B4. Beam me up!

Background Information:

A *grid* is a set of crossing vertical and horizontal lines used to locate places on a map. The lines form boxes that make it easier to describe a location on a map. *Rows* are the boxes arranged horizontally. *Columns* are the boxes arranged vertically.

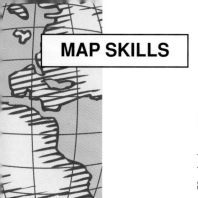

Introducing The Lesson:

Instruct students to gather around the grid on the floor. Have six student volunteers each hold a labeled sheet of construction paper. Direct each student with a numeral to sit beside a row. Then direct each student with a letter to sit above a column as shown. Keep the letters and numerals in order.

Steps:

1. Stand in one of the boxes. Ask a volunteer to describe where you are standing. Accept any reasonable response. Then share the Background Information on page 39.

2. Explain that the letters and numbers work together to determine a specific box on the grid. Point to the child in your column and to the child in your row. Have the pair hold up their cards. Announce the coordinates.

3. Stand in a different box and repeat Step 2 until students have an understanding of how the grid works. Then have students return to their seats.

4. Distribute a copy of page 41 to each child.

5. Review the directions at the top of the page. Reinforce the use of the grid by asking where the space traveler would go for shuttle repairs and confirm the response *(to the garage in E2)*. Have students complete the page independently.

6. Challenge students to complete the Bonus Box activity.

Using a grid

Blasting Off With Grids

Space traveler Red E. Tolaunch has just landed at Sparky's Space Station. She plans to run a few errands and get some much needed rest before she blasts off to another galaxy. However, Red needs help with her map. Use the grid to write the location of each place on Red's list.

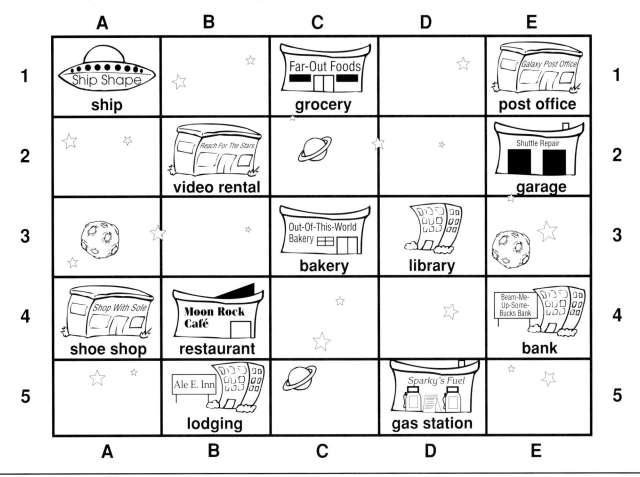

List Of Errands

1. Return the book *No Longer Lost In Space* to Stellar Library. _____
2. Pick up mail at the Galaxy Post Office. _____
3. Eat a fine meal at Moon Rock Café. _____
4. Pick up some groceries at Far-Out Foods. _____
5. Get some cash at Beam-Me-Up-Some-Bucks Bank. _____
6. Enjoy some donuts at Out-Of-This-World Bakery. _____
7. Have the hole in my spaceshoe repaired at Shop With Sole. _____
8. Get a good night's sleep at Ale E. Inn. _____
9. I need to return something at B2. What could it be? _____
10. Oh, no! Where did I park my spaceship, *Ship Shape?* _____

Bonus Box: Red forgot to write down something she needs! She can't blast off without it! Look at the map. On the back of this paper, write what Red needs to get and where she can get it.

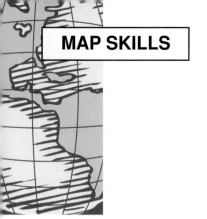

How To Extend The Lesson:

- Invite students to add a creative touch to their grid practice. In advance, create a 10 x 10 grid and duplicate a copy for each student, plus one extra. On the extra grid create a simple design similar to the one shown below. Then, on the chalkboard, make a list of the boxes that have been filled in to create the design. To complete the activity, each student refers to the list and colors the appropriate boxes on her grid. After each student has completed her design, post the original design for students to check their papers. If desired, duplicate extra copies of the blank grid and encourage each student to create her own design, list the boxes to color, and then ask a classmate to solve it.

- Using a grid pattern such as the one suggested above, instruct students to design a playground. Have each student draw playground equipment in the boxes of his choice. Then have students exchange papers and write the location of each piece of equipment.

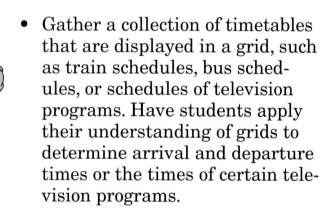

- Gather a collection of timetables that are displayed in a grid, such as train schedules, bus schedules, or schedules of television programs. Have students apply their understanding of grids to determine arrival and departure times or the times of certain television programs.

- Use a globe or map of the world to show how latitude and longitude lines create a grid. Have students locate different countries using these lines.

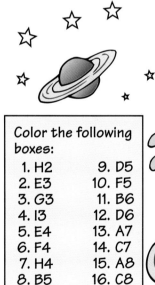

Color the following boxes:

1. H2	9. D5
2. E3	10. F5
3. G3	11. B6
4. I3	12. D6
5. E4	13. A7
6. F4	14. C7
7. H4	15. A8
8. B5	16. C8

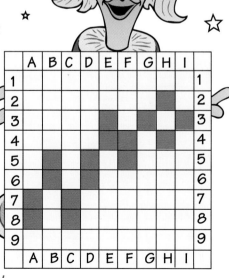

Homegrown

Students discover that product maps are a picture-perfect learning tool with this lesson!

Skill: Analyzing a product map

Estimated Lesson Time: 30 minutes

Teacher Preparation:
1. Duplicate page 45 for each student.
2. Cut out or draw several pictures of well-known agricultural products, such as oranges, coconuts, rice, or maple syrup.

Materials:
1 copy of page 45 for each student
several pictures of well-known agricultural products
a large United States and/or world map (optional)
crayons (optional)

Background Information:
A product map uses symbols to show the location of the most important products of an area. Symbols are explained in the map key.

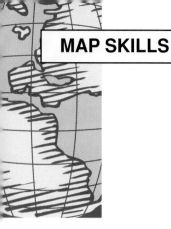

Introducing The Lesson:

Begin the lesson by displaying the pictures of well-known agricultural products. Ask students to guess where the products were grown. Accept all reasonable responses.

Steps:

1. Share the Background Information on page 43. Then distribute a copy of page 45 to each student. Explain to students that the reproducible shows a product map of an area where people make a living raising crops.

2. Instruct each student to locate the map key on her reproducible. Call on student volunteers to share the information found in the map key. If desired, have students lightly color each symbol (both in the key and on the map) a different color to help distinguish between them.

3. Guide students in understanding that a product map gives us information about the crops of an area and gives clues as to the types of jobs available there. For example, the types of jobs available where oranges are grown might include farming, orange picking, and making orange juice or orange marmalade.

4. Review the directions at the top of the page and have each student complete the page independently.

5. Challenge students to complete the Bonus Box activity.

Name _____

Homegrown

Read the questions below.
Then use the product map to help answer the questions.
Write your answers on the lines.

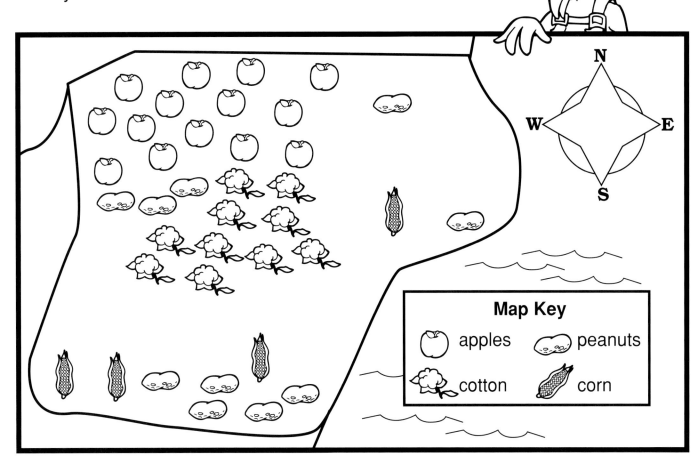

1. What is used to show products on a map? _____
2. How many different products are shown on the map? _____
3. Which product is grown the most? _____
4. In how many different places are peanuts grown? _____
5. Which product is found the most in the northern part of the state? _____
6. Which two products are grown in the southern part of the state? _____
   _____
7. Which product is grown in the north, south, east, and west of the state?
   _____
8. Which crops are grown in the center of the state? _____
9. Which crop is grown as much as cotton? _____
10. Which product probably brings in the least amount of money? _____
    Why? _____

Bonus Box: On the back of this paper, list three jobs that might be found in this state.

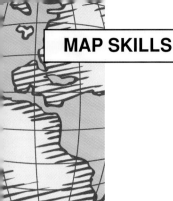

How To Extend The Lesson:

- Have students create their own product maps with this engaging lesson. For each of several small groups, draw a large outline of your state on a sheet of tagboard. Then provide each group with a state outline, crayons, and reference materials containing product information about your state. Then instruct each group to create a product map within the state outline that shows the important agricultural areas. Instruct each group to include a key on its product map. Post the completed maps on a classroom wall for everyone to see.

- Arrange a field trip to a place where an important agricultural or industrial product is made in your town. Have students observe the different types of jobs available due to the type of product grown or made. When you return to the classroom, direct each student to write a paragraph explaining the importance of the product to the local community.

- Help students understand that more than just agricultural products can be shown on a product map. Show students a product's label that tells where it was made, such as a sweater. Then ask each student to bring in something from another country. Provide time for each student to share his product and tell which country it was made in; then help him locate its origin on a world map. Write the name of the product on a sticky note and post it on the map. After everyone has shared, discuss the information on the map.

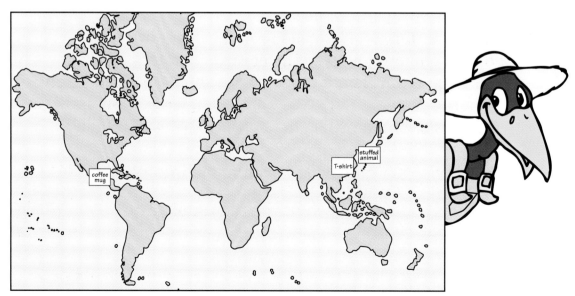

Analyzing a product map

A Bird's-Eye View Of Geography

Take students' understanding of geographic terms to new heights with this high-flying lesson!

Skill: Identifying and describing geographic terms

Estimated Lesson Time: 45 minutes

Teacher Preparation:
1. Duplicate page 49 and the bird's-eye view diagram on page 50 for each student.
2. Cut out ten construction-paper fish. On each fish, write one of the geographic terms listed in the Background Information below.

Materials:
1 copy of page 49 and the bird's-eye view diagram on page 50 for each student
10 construction-paper fish labeled with geographic terms
tape

Background Information:
The earth is covered with a variety of land and water features. Some of the features are:
ocean—a large body of salt water
coast—the land next to the ocean
harbor—a place on a coast where ships can dock safely
gulf—a large area of ocean partly surrounded by land
bay—a small area of ocean partly surrounded by land
island—land completely surrounded by water
peninsula—a piece of land with water on three sides of it
river—a large stream of water
delta—the land formed at the mouth of a river
mouth of river—the place where a river empties into a larger body of water

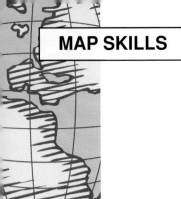

Introducing The Lesson:

On the chalkboard, draw a pelican with a large bill like the one shown below. Then draw a wavy line across the board to indicate water and tape the ten construction-paper fish below it. Announce to students that "Big Bill," a very hungry pelican, is ready for a snack! Explain that they will catch fish for him.

Steps:

1. Give each student a copy of the bird's-eye view diagram on page 50. To have students catch a fish for Big Bill, read a definition of one of the terms from the Background Information (page 47). Then ask a volunteer to take down the fish that is labeled with the word that matches the definition. If the student selects the correct word, he tapes the fish in the pelican's bill. If the student's choice is incorrect, he returns the fish to the ocean and tries again. After a correct response, have each student write the term on the appropriate line on his diagram. Continue in this manner until all the fish have been fed to Big Bill.

2. Give each student a copy of page 49. Review the directions and have each student complete the page independently.

3. Challenge students to complete the Bonus Box activity.

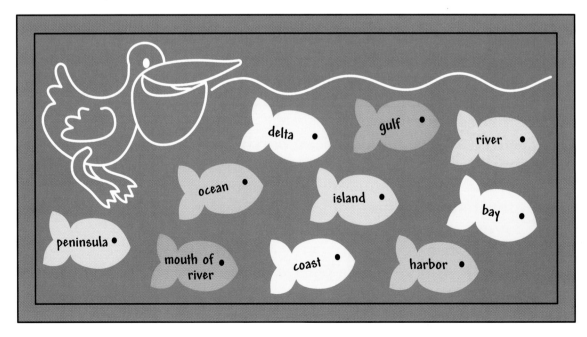

Identifying and describing geographic terms

A Bird's-Eye View Of Geography

Read each definition in Big Bill's bill.
Find the fish with the matching word.
Write the fish's letter on the blank.

1. _____ a piece of land with water on three sides of it
2. _____ a large area of ocean partly surrounded by land
3. _____ a small area of ocean partly surrounded by land
4. _____ a large stream of water
5. _____ a large body of salt water
6. _____ the place where a river empties into a larger body of water
7. _____ the land next to an ocean
8. _____ land completely surrounded by water
9. _____ a place on a coast where ships can dock safely
10. _____ the land formed at the mouth of a river

A. ocean
B. peninsula
C. bay
D. harbor
E. island
F. mouth of river
G. coast
H. gulf
I. delta
J. river

Fill in each blank below with the correct word. Use the words listed on the fish.
1. Airplane is to airport as boat is to _____.
2. Moat is to castle as water is to _____.
3. Cupcake is to cake as bay is to _____.

Bonus Box: On the back of this paper, write a sentence describing the differences between each of the following:
1. peninsula and island
2. bay and gulf

49

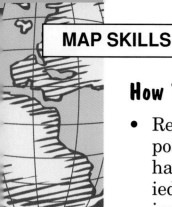

How To Extend The Lesson:

- Reinforce your study of geographic terms by having students create postcards. Give each student a 4" x 6" index card. On the unlined side, have each student color a picture of one of the natural features studied. Then direct the student to turn her card over and write about an imaginary visit to the area, being sure to include the name of the natural feature and a description. Next have her address her card to a classmate before delivering it to him or her.

- Use this center activity to review geographic terms and encourage critical thinking. Create a set of vocabulary cards with the geographic terms studied. Place the cards, a supply of paper, a pencil, and two Hula Hoop® rings at a center. To complete the activity, a student places the rings on the floor next to each other. Then he determines classifications for some of the words, such as land versus water, large versus small, or coastal versus inland. Next he places the cards with words that fit one classification into one ring and the cards with words that fit the other classification into the other ring. Then he writes down the different classifications and the corresponding geographic terms. When finished, he shares his lists with a classmate.

Bird's-Eye View

Use with Step 1 on page 48.

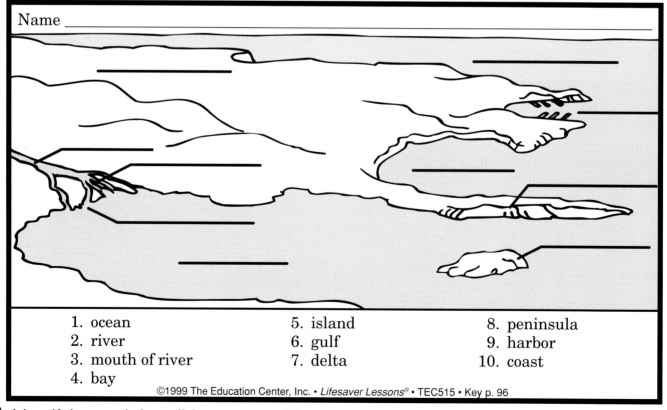

Name _____

1. ocean	5. island	8. peninsula
2. river	6. gulf	9. harbor
3. mouth of river	7. delta	10. coast
4. bay		

Identifying and describing geographic terms

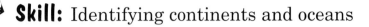

Where In The World?

Send students searching for the earth's continents and oceans with this worldly lesson.

> **Skill:** Identifying continents and oceans

Estimated Lesson Time: 30 minutes

Teacher Preparation:
1. Duplicate page 53 for each student.
2. Use the chart below to label each of 11 index cards.

Front Of Card	Back Of Card
North America	suitcase
South America	hat
Europe	umbrella
Asia	alarm clock
Antarctica	boots
Africa	backpack
Australia	toothbrush
Atlantic Ocean	swimming trunks
Pacific Ocean	suntan lotion
Indian Ocean	sunglasses
Arctic Ocean	socks

Materials:
1 copy of page 53 for each student
11 index cards labeled with continents and oceans
crayons

Background Information:
The earth's large land areas are called *continents*. There are seven continents. They are North America, South America, Europe, Asia, Antarctica, Africa, and Australia.

Our world has four oceans. They are the Atlantic, the Pacific, the Indian, and the Arctic. The largest is the Pacific Ocean and the smallest is the Arctic Ocean.

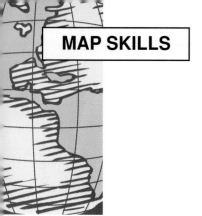

Introducing The Lesson:

Ask students if they have ever lost anything while traveling. Provide time for students to tell briefly about some of their experiences. Then distribute a copy of page 53 to each student. Tell students that Grizz Lee Bear is a world-traveling bear who has lost many personal possessions on his journeys. Assign the class the task of helping Grizz Lee Bear find them.

Steps:

1. Choose one of the programmed index cards and read aloud the item (not the continent or ocean). Instruct each student to look at her world map on the reproducible and find where Grizz Lee Bear left it. When students have located the item on the map, ask if anyone can name the continent or ocean where it was found. Confirm the answer or provide it by showing the other side of the card. Then instruct each student to label the continent or ocean on her map. Continue in this manner until all continents and oceans have been identified and labeled. If desired, encourage students to lightly color their maps to distinguish between the continents and oceans.

2. Refer students to the compass rose on their maps and review cardinal directions. Then have a volunteer read the directions below the map. Instruct each student to complete the page independently.

3. Challenge students to complete the Bonus Box activity.

Where In The World?

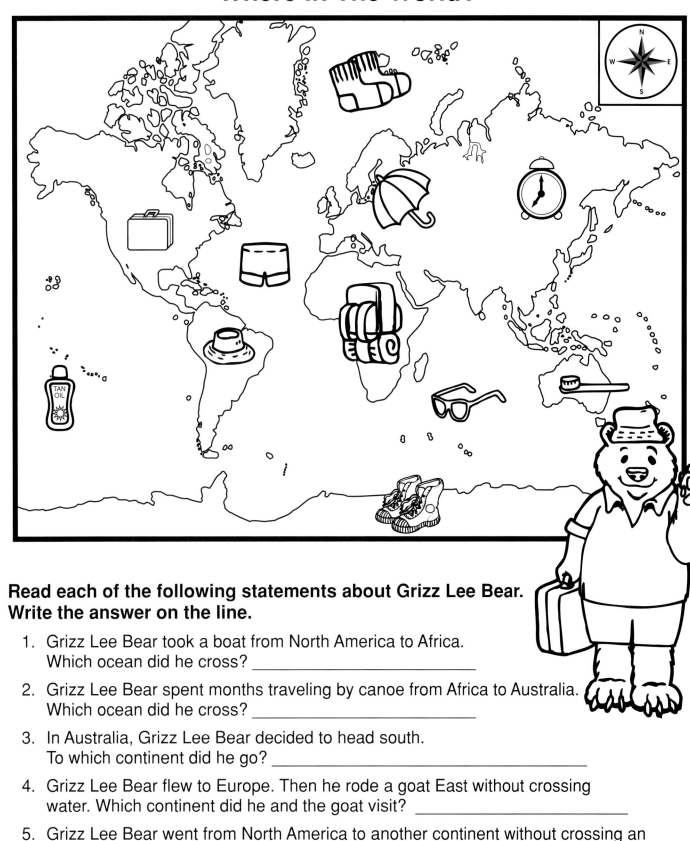

Read each of the following statements about Grizz Lee Bear. Write the answer on the line.

1. Grizz Lee Bear took a boat from North America to Africa.
   Which ocean did he cross? _____

2. Grizz Lee Bear spent months traveling by canoe from Africa to Australia.
   Which ocean did he cross? _____

3. In Australia, Grizz Lee Bear decided to head south.
   To which continent did he go? _____

4. Grizz Lee Bear flew to Europe. Then he rode a goat East without crossing
   water. Which continent did he and the goat visit? _____

5. Grizz Lee Bear went from North America to another continent without crossing an
   ocean. To which continent did he travel? _____

Bonus Box: On the back of this paper, write the names of two continents that are joined.

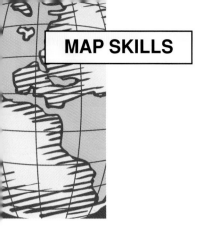

How To Extend The Lesson:

• Display a large world map. Then pair students and assign each twosome a continent or ocean. Instruct each pair to write a riddle about its assigned geographical feature on a sheet of paper. (For example: The Atlantic Ocean and the Indian Ocean touch me. Europe is north of me. Who am I? *[Africa]*) Have students write the answer to the riddle at the bottom of their papers. When students have completed their riddles, collect them and read each one aloud. Challenge student volunteers to determine the answers to the riddles and point to the geographical feature on the map.

• Assign each student a continent or ocean. Provide reference materials, such as encyclopedias, and have the student find several facts about his topic. Then have the student make an acrostic like the one shown that incorporates some of the facts. Invite students to decorate their completed work; then display the acrostics on a bulletin board titled "Words Of The World!"

• Use this center idea to motivate youngsters to practice identifying continents and oceans. Enlarge one copy of the map on page 53. If desired, color and laminate it. With a marker, label 11 pinch clothespins with a different continent or ocean. Place the map, clothespins, and the labeled index cards used for the lesson on page 52 at the center. To complete the activity, the student matches a labeled clothespin to its corresponding continent or ocean on the map (see the illustration on this page). Once all of the clothespins are standing, the student checks his answers against the index cards.

LOTS OF FISH
TOUCHES ANTARCTICA
THIRD LARGEST OCEAN
TOUCHES ASIA
LARGE WATER AREA
POLLUTION PROBLEM

ONE OF FOUR OCEANS
TOUCHES AUSTRALIA
EQUATOR RUNS THROUGH IT
TOUCHES AFRICA
LOTS OF ANIMALS

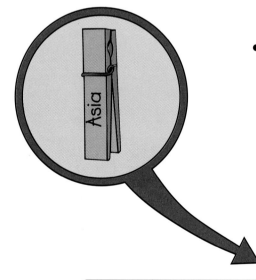

Asia

Going The Distance With Scales

Students will measure up with this map-scale lesson.

Skill: Using a scale to determine distance

Estimated Lesson Time: 30 minutes

Teacher Preparation:
Duplicate page 57 for
each student.

Materials:
1 copy of page 57 for
   each student
1 globe
1 centimeter ruler
   for each student
scissors
glue

Background Information:
   Maps are used to represent real places on the earth's surface. For
a map to be manageable, the places and distances shown must be
smaller than their actual sizes. For a map to be useful, it must show
the correct size of an area and the correct distances between places.
   Bar scales are included on maps to help the user determine distances. A bar scale uses a standard unit of measurement, such as an
inch, to stand for a certain number of miles or kilometers.

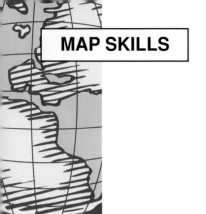

Introducing The Lesson:

Ask students how long it might take to travel all the way around the earth. Discuss the different modes of transportation one might use and which might be fastest. Next proclaim that you can travel around the world in less than one minute. Then place a globe in the front of the room and walk around it.

Steps:

1. Remind students that the globe is a scaled-down model of the earth. Discuss how the landforms on the globe are the correct shapes and distances from one another, but smaller.

Bar Scale

0   1

1 inch = 1 mile

2. Ask students to explain the differences between a globe and a map. Accept reasonable responses, such as a globe is like a ball and a map is flat. Then share the Background Information on page 55 with students.

3. Draw a simple bar scale on the chalkboard (see the example at the left). Explain to students that map scales help people determine distances between places.

4. Distribute centimeter rulers, scissors, glue, and a copy of page 57 to each student. Tell students that Marty Mountaineer is vacationing at Grande National Park but his map is incomplete. Marty needs their help filling in the missing information. Read the directions aloud and, if desired, complete the first clue together. Then have students complete the page independently.

5. Challenge students to complete the Bonus Box activity.

Using a scale to determine distance

Name_____

Going The Distance With Scales

Color and cut out the pictures at the bottom of the page.
Then read each clue below.
Use the compass rose, map scale, and centimeter ruler
   to decide where each picture belongs.
Glue the picture in place.

1 cm = 1 mile

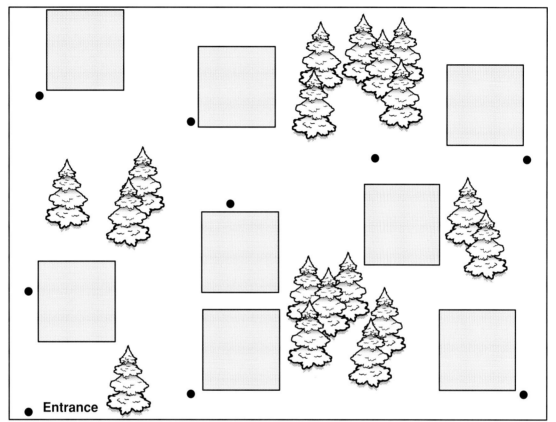

Entrance

Bonus Box: On the back of this page, write the names of two places on the map. Then write how many miles apart they are.

1. Grassy Meadow is 3 miles north of the entrance sign.

2. Lookout Cliff is 5 miles north of Grassy Meadow.

3. Wild River is 4 miles east of Lookout Cliff.

4. Spring Lake is 7 miles south of Wild River.

5. Dark Cavern is 9 miles east of Spring Lake.

6. The Grande Mountains are 6 miles north of Dark Cavern.

7. Green Forest is 4 miles west of the Grande Mountains.

8. The Ranger Station is 4 miles southwest of Green Forest.

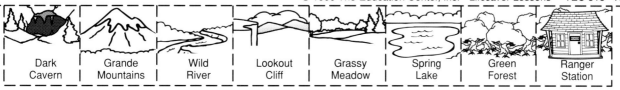

| Dark Cavern | Grande Mountains | Wild River | Lookout Cliff | Grassy Meadow | Spring Lake | Green Forest | Ranger Station |

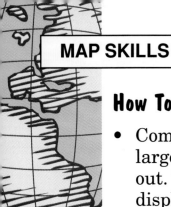

How To Extend The Lesson:

- Combine motivation and map scales with this incentive program. Enlarge a copy of Marty Mountaineer (shown below); color it and cut it out. Then draw a simple mountain shape on bulletin-board paper and display it on a classroom wall. Below the mountain, post the map scale 1 inch = 10 feet. Also post a sign that names the behavior you would like students to demonstrate, such as walking quietly in the halls. Then tell students that each time you see the featured behavior, you will move Marty ten feet up the mountain. If students behave especially well, have Marty climb an extra ten feet. Celebrate reaching the summit with a popcorn treat.

- Have students make a map of the classroom with this hands-on activity. Give each student a piece of half-inch graph paper, a ruler, and a pencil. Using a tape measure, determine the length and width of the classroom in feet. Have students draw the perimeter of the classroom on their papers, each square representing one foot. Then have students measure items in the room, such as desks, tables, and bookshelves. Instruct students to add the items to their maps, keeping them to scale.

- For a personal twist to learning about map scales, have students measure themselves. Using the scale 1 inch = 1 foot, have pairs of students measure each other from head to foot. Instruct each student to round her height to the nearest foot and draw a scaled-down version of herself. Below each picture, have the student copy and complete the following sentence: "[Name] would be ____ inches tall." Display the pictures under the caption "If A Foot Were An Inch..."

Using a scale to determine distance

Comparing Communities

Journey across the earth to investigate Vietnam with this world-class lesson.

Skill: Investigating a community in another area of the world.

Estimated Lesson Time: 35 minutes

Teacher Preparation:
Duplicate page 61 for each student.

Materials:
1 copy of page 61 for each student
world map

Background Information:

Vietnam is a country in Southeast Asia. Vietnamese is the official language of Vietnam. Most people in Vietnam live in villages near rivers or along the coast. Many Vietnamese fish for a living or raise rice. The main diet of the Vietnamese is fish, rice, and vegetables. The bicycle is an important form of transportation in Vietnam. Very few Vietnamese own a car.

Different styles of clothing are worn in Vietnam. Some Vietnamese wear styles similar to those worn in the United States. Other Vietnamese people may wear black trousers and tightly buttoned white or dark-colored jackets. Still others may wear loose-fitting trousers and long-sleeved shirts.

The materials used to build homes in Vietnam depend on the part of the country where the homes are built. In the north where it is cooler, homes are made of wood or bamboo and might have tiled roofs. In the south where it is warm, homes are usually built with walls and roofs made of palm leaves or straw. There are some families who live on the water in fishing boats. Some homes in rural areas have no electricity.

Introducing The Lesson:

Ask students to brainstorm words or phrases that describe their community's climate, natural resources, and industry. Record youngsters' ideas on the chalkboard. Ask them if people in other communities would use these same words or phrases to describe their own communities. Guide students to understand that communities have many similarities and differences.

Steps:

1. On a large world map, have one child locate Vietnam. Then share with youngsters the Background Information on page 59.

2. Write the headings "Similarities" and "Differences" on the chalkboard (see the illustration). Then guide a class discussion on the similarities and differences between their community and a community in Vietnam based on the Background Information. Write student responses under the appropriate heading.

3. When students show a good understanding of the similarities and differences between the two communities, give each student a copy of page 61. Ask a volunteer to read aloud the information and directions at the top of the page. Have each student complete the page independently.

Similarities
Both communities have transportation.

People work in both communities.

Clothing is sometimes similar.

Differences
Many people in our community work in factories.

Many people in Vietnam fish or work in rice fields.

Many homes in our community are made of brick or aluminum siding.

Vietnamese homes are made of wood, bamboo, straw, or palm leaves.

Name _____

Comparing Communities

Read each heading.

Study the home, food, and transportation of the community in Vietnam shown below.

Then, in the boxes below, draw pictures to show a home, food, and transportation for your community.

On the lines, write the similarities and differences between the two communities.

A Community In Vietnam

Home	Food	Transportation
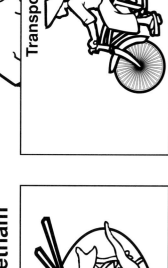		

Your Community

Home	Food	Transportation

_____

_____

_____

_____

OUR
NEIGHBORS

How To Extend The Lesson:

- Challenge students to use encyclopedias to research other communities, such as Mexico City, Moscow, and Tokyo. Have each youngster write a short report about the community. Direct the child to include the community's size, natural resources, and types of transportation and homes. Then have the student use a Venn diagram to compare the community she lives in to the community in her report.

- Have youngsters make travel posters inviting tourists to visit their community or another community studied in class. To do this, give each student a 9" x 12" sheet of white construction paper. Have him write a catchy title at the top of the paper, such as "Take A Bite Out Of The Big Apple!" or "Bet You'll Love Boyertown!" Next, on the top half of the paper, direct the child to write three sentences explaining why the community would be a great place to visit. On the bottom half, have him draw a landscape that represents the community. Display the posters in your hallway.

- Tell students that a special community committee would like them to write newspaper articles stating the positive aspects of living in two selected communities. Have half of your students write and illustrate an article about the community they live in, and have the other half write and illustrate an article about a community in Vietnam. To publish the students' works, mount the projects on a series of newspaper pages. Decorate the front page of the newspaper to show the title "Special Communities," the date, and a class byline. Laminate the pages for durability; then place the publication in your class library.

Hip, Hip, Holidays!

Give students something to cheer about with this lesson on religious and nonreligious holidays!

Skill: Distinguishing between religious and nonreligious holidays

Estimated Lesson Time: 30 minutes

Teacher Preparation:
Duplicate page 65 for each student.

Materials:
1 copy of page 65 for each student
scissors
glue

Background Information:
A *holiday* is any day people set aside their ordinary duties to celebrate. Originally, holidays honored religious events and holy people. Religious holidays include Christmas, Easter, and Hanukkah. Today we also celebrate holidays that are not religious. Nonreligious holidays include Flag Day, Father's Day, and Thanksgiving.

<u>**Religious Holidays**</u>
Passover
Good Friday
Easter
Rosh Hashanah
Yom Kippur
All Saints' Day
Hanukkah
Ramadan
Christmas

<u>**Nonreligious Holidays**</u>
New Year's Day
Martin Luther King Jr.'s Birthday
Groundhog Day
Abraham Lincoln's Birthday
George Washington's Birthday
Mother's Day
Memorial Day
Flag Day
Father's Day
Independence Day
Columbus Day
Veterans Day
Thanksgiving

Introducing The Lesson:

Invite students to name their favorite holidays. Write their responses on the chalkboard.

Steps:

1. Share the Background Information on page 63 with students. Referring to the list on the chalkboard, have students determine if each holiday is religious or not religious. Place an *N* next to the holidays that are not religious and an *R* next to the ones that are religious.

2. Distribute scissors, glue, and a copy of page 65 to each student.

3. Have a student volunteer read the directions aloud. Then have students complete the page independently.

4. Challenge students to complete the Bonus Box activity.

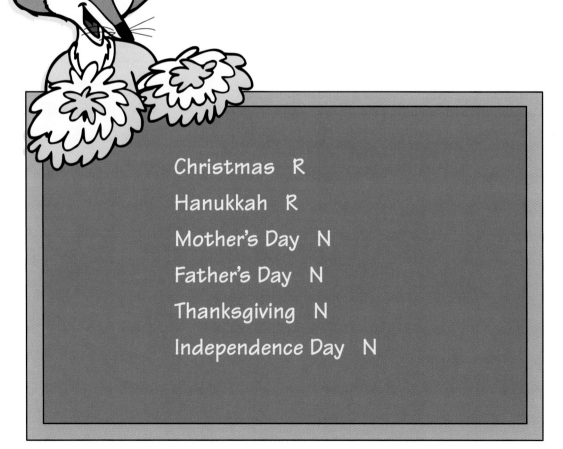

Christmas   R

Hanukkah   R

Mother's Day   N

Father's Day   N

Thanksgiving   N

Independence Day   N

Distinguishing between religious and nonreligious holidays

Name_____

Hip, Hip, Holidays!

Cut out the boxes at the bottom of the page.
Then read about the holidays.
Decide if the holiday is religious or not religious.
Glue the name in the correct column next to its matching holiday.

Holiday	Religious	Not Religious
1. A holiday to take time and give thanks		
2. A holiday to honor mothers		
3. A holiday to celebrate Columbus landing in the New World		
4. A Christian holiday that honors the birth of Jesus		
5. A holiday to celebrate the first day of the new year		
6. A holiday to honor St. Patrick, the patron saint of Ireland		
7. A holiday to honor the U.S. flag		
8. A holiday to honor fathers		
9. A Jewish holiday also known as the Festival of Lights		
10. A holiday to honor the Declaration of Independence		

Bonus Box: On the back of this page, list two more religious holidays and two more nonreligious holidays.

Columbus Day	Father's Day	Christmas	St. Patrick's Day	Hanukkah	Mother's Day	Independence Day	Flag Day	New Year's Day	Thanksgiving

How To Extend The Lesson:

- Continue your study of religious and nonreligious holidays for the remainder of the school year. To do this, post a large calendar prominently on a classroom wall. Then, as the calendar is changed each month, discuss each upcoming holiday with students and have them determine whether it is religious or nonreligious. On the calendar, write *religious* or *not religious* on the appropriate date.

- Challenge students to find out about religious and nonreligious holidays celebrated in other countries. Ask each child to choose a holiday that she would like to research. Then provide students with encyclopedias and books about holidays in other countries. Give students time to read about their holidays. Next, on a sheet of drawing paper, have each student provide information about her holiday. Instruct her to include the name of the holiday, the country in which it is celebrated, a description of the festivities, whether it is religious or nonreligious, and an illustration. Then post the completed projects on a bulletin board titled "Holidays Around The World!"

- Enlist the help of students to create a matching game to place in a classroom center. On one side of a blank index card, write the name of a holiday. On another blank card, write a description of the holiday. Using different holidays, repeat this procedure until you have a deck of several game cards. Once the cards have been completed, place them in a resealable plastic bag and set them in the center. To play the game, two to four students shuffle and deal all of the cards. The first player randomly pulls a card from the hand of another player. If the card corresponds with one in his hand, he sets down the two matching cards and takes another turn. If he does not have the corresponding card, he keeps the card and the next player takes her turn. The game is over when all cards have been matched. The player with the most pairs wins the game. At the end of the game, have students sort their cards into religious and nonreligious piles.

Thanksgiving

This federal holiday is celebrated on the fourth Thursday in November. It is a day to give thanks.

Terrific U.S. Timelines

Uncle Sam would agree—this timeline lesson is just what you need to teach your youngsters how to sequence important U.S. events!

Skill: Sequencing major events in United States history on a timeline

Estimated Lesson Time: 30 minutes

Teacher Preparation:
1. Duplicate page 69 for each student.
2. Label each of eight strips of paper with a historical U.S. event and its date (see the sample list on this page).
3. Place the strips in a container, such as a small paper bag or envelope.
4. Draw a timeline from 1620–1970 on the chalkboard in ten-year increments.

Materials:
1 copy of page 69 for each student
1 sheet of blank paper for each student
8 programmed paper strips
container
scissors
glue
tape

Pilgrims landed in America
1620

Declaration of Independence adopted
1776

U.S. Constitution signed
1787

Settlers began following the Oregon Trail
1841

Civil War began
1861

Henry Ford produced the Model T car
1908

World War I ended
1918

Martin Luther King Jr. received the Nobel Peace Prize
1964

Background Information:
A timeline is a line that shows a number of years. It marks events in the order they happened.

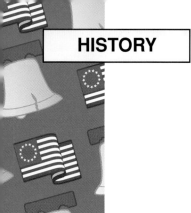

Introducing The Lesson:

Have students use their bodies to create a timeline of their birthdays. First have each child write her birthday on a sheet of blank paper. Then have her tape her paper to the front of her clothing so that the date can be read. Next announce "January." Have students with January birthdays line up at the front of the classroom starting at the far left. Then announce "February." Have youngsters with February birthdays line up to the right of students with January birthdays. Continue in this manner until you have called out each month in sequential order. Next have students who were born within the same month arrange themselves in chronological order based on their birthdays. Point out to students that they have just completed a timeline of class birthdays. Then tell them that they will also be arranging the dates of U.S. events using a timeline.

Steps:

1. Share with students the Background Information on page 67. Then refer them to the timeline on the chalkboard.

2. Have a student volunteer take a paper strip from the container. Instruct her to read aloud the historical event and the date. Help the child tape the strip to the appropriate location on the timeline. Continue in this manner until all of the strips have been correctly placed on the timeline.

3. Give each student a copy of page 69, scissors, and glue. Have a volunteer read aloud the directions at the top of the page. Then have each student complete the assignment independently.

Name _____

Terrific U.S. Timelines

Directions:

1. Cut out each timeline section. Glue the sections together as indicated.
2. Cut out the event boxes.
3. For each event, find its matching date on the timeline. Then glue the box above its date.
4. Draw an arrow from the timeline date to the event.

Events

First man walked on the Moon 1969	California Gold Rush 1849	Trans-continental Railroad finished 1869	First airplane flight 1903	Women given right to vote 1920	Revolutionary War began 1775	George Washington elected president 1789	Statue of Liberty given to the U.S. 1884

Timeline Pattern

1770	1780	1790	1800	1810	1820	1830	1840	1850	1860	18

70	1880	1890	1900	1910	1920	1930	1940	1950	1960	1970

Glue to 18

69

How To Extend The Lesson:

- Assign each student a different U.S. historical event (see the list below). Provide resource books for students to research the events. Give each student a 9" x 12" sheet of white construction paper. Then have the child write the year of her event on the top half of the paper. On the bottom half of the paper, have her draw a picture of the event. Instruct the child to write three sentences about the event on the back of her paper. Next direct each student who has a date in the 1800s to bring her paper to the front of the classroom. Have those students arrange themselves in chronological order. Continue in this manner for each century. Then have each student, in order, read aloud her three sentences. Post the completed projects on a classroom wall in sequential order to form a giant timeline.

- Have students practice timeline skills with this math activity. Write a list of U.S. events and their corresponding dates on the chalkboard (see the list below). Give each student a copy of the timeline pattern on page 69. Have him cut out the sections and glue them together to form a timeline. Then share with students addition and subtraction clues, such as "This event happened 61 years before Abraham Lincoln became the 16th U.S. president" *(Washington, DC, became the nation's capital)*. Have each student write the event above the matching date on his timeline. Continue in this manner until you have shared a clue for each event.

- Learning and fun are sure to unfold with this class timeline book! Assign each student a different U.S. historical event (see the list below). Have each student use resource books to research her event. Next have the child turn a 6" x 9" sheet of white construction paper horizontally, draw a picture related to her event, and write the event and date at the bottom of the page. Under your students' direction, arrange the completed pages in chronological order. Label a construction paper cover with the title "Our Terrific Timeline" and illustrate it. Tape the sides of the pages together as shown and fold the book accordion-style. Place the completed book in your classroom library.

U.S. Historical Events
Washington, DC, became the nation's capital. (1800)
Harriet Tubman organized the Underground Railroad. (1850)
Abraham Lincoln became the 16th U.S. president. (1861)
Alexander Graham Bell invented the telephone. (1876)
Clara Barton founded the American Red Cross. (1881)
Hawaii became the 50th state. (1959)

Sequencing events on a timeline

Then And Now

Teach students that communities change over time with this look at the past.

Skill: Identifying changes in a community

Estimated Lesson Time: 30 minutes

Teacher Preparation:
Duplicate page 73 for each student.

Materials:
1 copy of page 73 per student

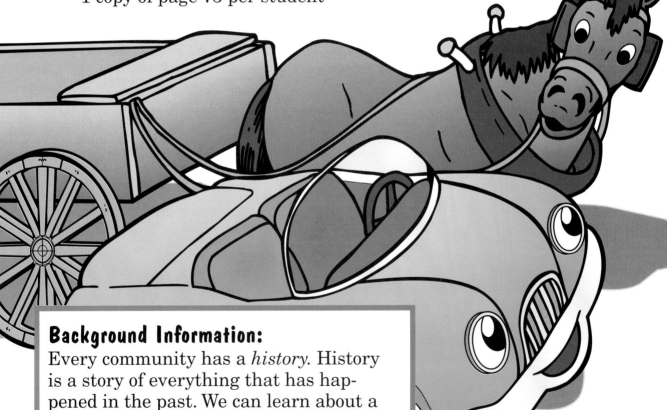

Background Information:
Every community has a *history*. History is a story of everything that has happened in the past. We can learn about a community's past by visiting libraries, museums, historical sites, and landmarks. We can also learn about the past by talking to people who remember things that happened a long time ago.

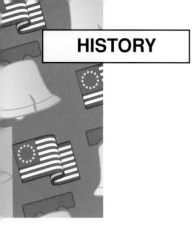

Introducing The Lesson:

Ask students to name things that change. Accept reasonable responses such as tadpoles changing into frogs or tree leaves changing colors. Then ask students how their community has changed in the last year or two. Encourage discussion about roads or homes being built in their neighborhoods or new stores that have opened in their community.

Steps:

1. Explain to students that the changes they have seen have been over a short period of time. Then explain to students that their community has changed a great deal during the last century. Share the Background Information on page 71 with students.

2. Explain to students that long ago things were quite different in their community. Ask students to imagine what their community might have been like before there was electricity. Guide a discussion about what clothing, shelter, transportation, and food were like long ago. List students' responses on the chalkboard.

3. Distribute a copy of page 73 to each student. Read the directions aloud. Next have students discuss what they think is happening in each picture at the bottom of the page. Then have students complete the page independently.

4. Challenge students to complete the Bonus Box activity.

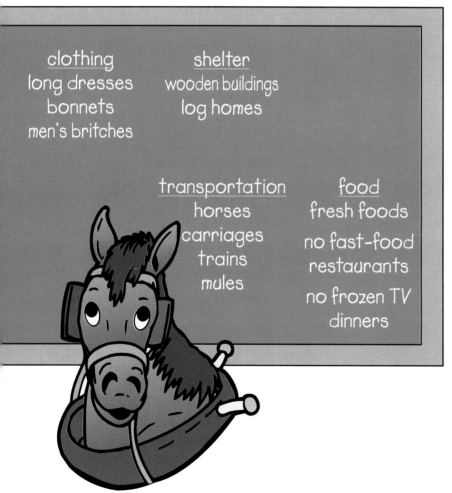

clothing
long dresses
bonnets
men's britches

shelter
wooden buildings
log homes

transportation
horses
carriages
trains
mules

food
fresh foods
no fast-food restaurants
no frozen TV dinners

Then And Now

Color and cut out the picture cards.
Put a drop of glue on each •. Glue the matching picture in place.

Then

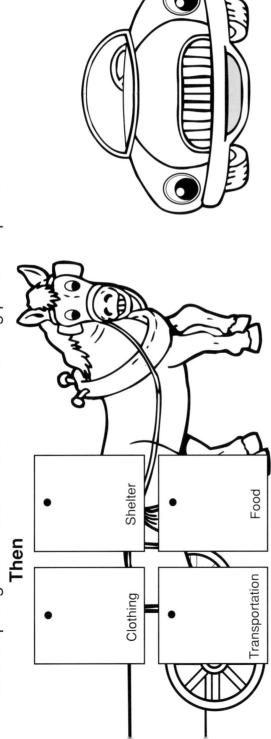

| • Shelter | • Clothing |
| • Food | • Transportation |

Now

| • Clothing | • Shelter |
| • Transportation | • Food |

On the lines below, write what you think your community
was like 200 years ago.

_____

_____

_____

On the lines below, write what your community is like
now.

_____

_____

_____

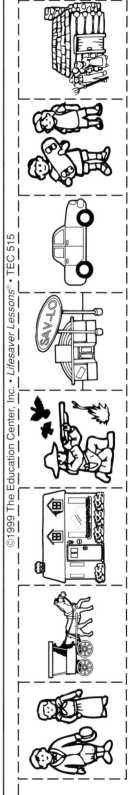

Bonus Box: On the back of this paper, draw a picture of what you think clothing, shelter, transportation, or food may look like in 100 years.

How To Extend The Lesson:

- To learn more about how their community has changed over time, have students interview older citizens. In advance, have students prepare a list of questions to ask, such as those shown below. Then have each student use her questions to interview a grandparent or other older citizen. Once the interviews have been completed, provide time for students to discuss what they have learned about their community. Follow up the activity by encouraging each student to write a thank-you note to the person she interviewed.

  - Are there any jobs that people once had that no longer exist?
  - What was it like when you went to school?
  - What seems to have changed the most?
  - As a child, what did you do for entertainment?

- Create a timeline of the important historical events of your community. Unroll a length of adding-machine paper. Draw a baseline and label evenly spaced dates at 20- or 50-year increments. Post the timeline in a prominent classroom location. As the class studies the history of its community and discovers an important historical event, label it on the timeline.

- Have students create dioramas that depict how their community looks today or how it looked in the past. Ask each student to bring from home a shoebox or other small box. To make his diorama, have each student use construction paper, glue, scissors, and other decorative items to create a present-day or historical scene of his community. Next have the student write a paragraph that tells about the scene he has created and glue it to the top or side of his diorama. Display the finished dioramas on a table for all to see.

Investigating Inventors

Send your young sleuths searching for facts about inventors with this information-packed lesson!

Skill: Identifying contributions of significant inventors

Estimated Lesson Time: 30 minutes

Teacher Preparation:
1. Duplicate page 77 for each student.
2. Make ten memory game cards. To do this, write the name of each inventor shown below on a large, blank index card. Then, for each inventor, draw a simple picture of his invention on another index card as shown. Mix up the cards; then turn them over and sequentially number them from 1 to 10.
3. In random order, tape each card to the chalkboard so that the numbered side is showing.

Materials:
1 copy of page 77 for each student
10 programmed index cards
tape

Alexander Graham Bell	Thomas Edison	Wilbur and Orville Wright	Benjamin Franklin	Henry Ford

Background Information:
Invention is the making of a new device, process, or product. Inventions, such as refrigerators and computers, can help make our lives easier and better. Some inventions, such as in-line skates and television, make life more fun.

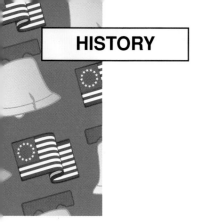

Introducing The Lesson:

Ask a student volunteer to select two cards, then turn over each card as its number is announced. If the two cards are a match (an inventor and his invention), take the cards down and set them side by side on the chalkboard ledge. If the cards do not match, turn the cards back over and invite another student volunteer to take a turn. Continue in this manner until all cards have been matched.

Steps:

1. Share the Background Information on page 75 with students. Encourage a class discussion about the usefulness of each invention revealed during the memory game. Then remove the cards from the chalkboard ledge.

2. Distribute a copy of page 77 to each student. Ask a student volunteer to read aloud the directions at the top of page 77. Then have students complete the page independently.

3. Challenge students to complete the Bonus Box activity.

Investigating Inventors

Read the clue below each box.
Find the matching inventor's name in the list of suspects.
Write the inventor's name (or names) on the line.
Then draw a picture of the invention in the square.

List Of Suspects
Alexander Graham Bell
Thomas Edison
Wilbur and Orville Wright
Benjamin Franklin
Henry Ford

1. **Clue:** I invented the thing that goes ring-a-ding-ding. Who am I?

2. **Clue:** We flew high and we flew low. Who are we?

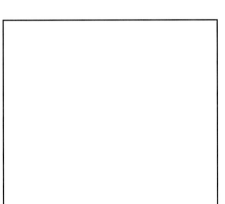

3. **Clue:** I was driven to produce a type of transportation for you. Who am I?

4. **Clue:** I light up your life with my bright invention. Who am I?

5. **Clue:** A lot of people focus on my invention. Who am I?

Bonus Box: On the back of this paper, write which invention is most important to you and why.

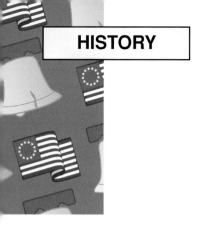

How To Extend The Lesson:

- Have each student write a thank-you letter to one of the inventors discussed in the lesson. Instruct the student to write why she likes his invention, how often she uses it, and what it would be like if it had never been invented. Once the writing assignment has been completed, encourage each student to read her letter to the class.

- Students will love piecing together these puzzling reports! Divide students into small groups and assign each group a famous inventor (see the list below). Using encyclopedias and books about inventors, each group researches interesting and important facts about its inventor and his invention. Next, instruct each group to draw a large illustration of the invention in the center of a sheet of poster board and write the inventor's name below it. Then have students write the facts they discovered around the illustration. Finally, have each group cut its poster board into large puzzle pieces and place the pieces in a large envelope. Have groups exchange envelopes and piece together one another's puzzles.

Homework Machine

Stacie

Homework Machine
I invented the homework machine to do all my homework. Now I have more time to play. This invention will do all your homework in five minutes. Talk into the microphone and tell it what to do. Wait a few minutes and the homework will shoot out the top.

James Watt—steam engine
Samuel Morse—telegraph
George Washington Carver—peanut products
Elias Howe—sewing machine
Whitcomb L. Judson—zipper
Garrett Morgan—three-color traffic light

- Give students an opportunity to solve problems and to be inventors. Guide each student to choose a problem that needs solving, such as pollution or flat tires. Then have the student think of an invention that would solve the problem. Direct each student to write a detailed description about his invention on a sheet of writing paper. Instruct the student to include the name of his invention, what it is used for, how it works, and why he invented it. Then, on a sheet of drawing paper, have the student illustrate his invention. When the projects have been completed, place each description on one-half of a bulletin board and each illustration on the other half. Title the display "Invention Match-Up!" Then encourage students to read each description and find its matching illustration during their free time.

Way Out West

Standard 14

*Send your youngsters time traveling with this
community services lesson.*

ervices of a community

Time: 30 minutes

)n:
for each student.

or each student

ition:
es services to meet the needs and wants of
inity manages fire and police departments
. The public works department provides clean
eats waste water, and collects garbage. A
services might include hospitals and clinics.
ices provide citizens with public transporta-
and trains. Public schools help citizens meet
ucation. To enhance the lives of its citizens,
le parks, museums, and libraries.

Introducing The Lesson:

On the chalkboard, draw a large cactus, a horizon line, and some distant mountains (see the illustration). Invite students to imagine that they have been transported back in time to a Wild West settlement. Explain that the settlement has homes and stores that meet their needs for food, clothing, and shelter. Then tell students that their new community does not provide other services they might want. Ask students what safety and recreational services they would like their new community to have. Accept reasonable responses, such as police, hospitals, and parks.

Steps:

1. Explain to students that people benefit from living in a community because it provides many services for its citizens. Then share the Background Information on page 79.

2. Distribute a copy of page 81, crayons, glue, and scissors to each student. Next have a volunteer read aloud the directions at the top of the page. Then instruct each student to complete the page independently.

3. Challenge students to complete the Bonus Box activity.

communities provide parks,

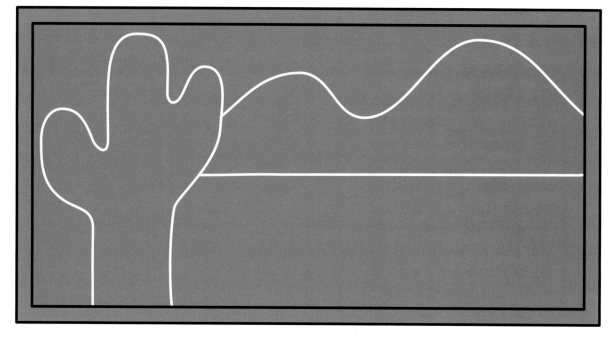

Name _____

Way Out West

Color and cut out the picture cards.
Read each service on the map.
Put a drop of glue on each •. Glue the matching picture in place.

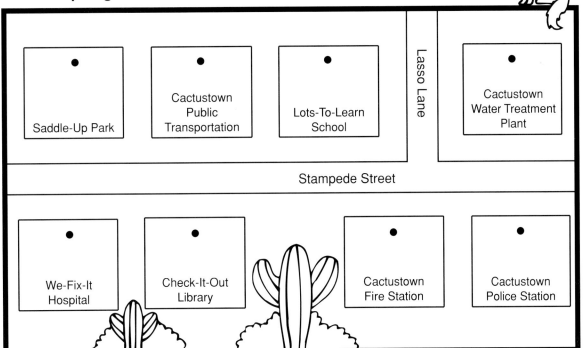

On the lines below, write the need that each service meets.

1. Saddle-Up Park _____

_____

2. Cactustown Public Transportation _____

_____

3. Lots-To-Learn School _____

_____

4. Cactustown Water Treatment Plant _____

_____

5. We-Fix-It Hospital _____

_____

6. Check-It-Out Library _____

_____

7. Cactustown Fire Station _____

_____

8. Cactustown Police Station _____

_____

How To Extend The Lesson:

• Put your community on display with this quilt activity. Have each child brainstorm the types of recreation in her community, such as lakes or roller rinks. Then instruct her to select a type of recreation and draw a picture of it on a nine-inch construction-paper square. Mount the completed squares on a length of bulletin-board paper to form a quilt. Use a marker to draw "stitches" around each square. Then display the quilt on a prominent wall and title it "Having Fun In Our Community!"

• Use this fun flip-book activity to explore the services of your community. To make a flip book, a student stacks two sheets of drawing paper; then holds the bottom piece in place and slides the top sheet upward to create two graduated layers. He folds both papers forward to create four graduated layers. Next the child staples the resulting booklet close to the fold. Each student titles the first layer "What My Community Provides," and then labels a layer for each of the following categories: Safety, Recreation, and Education (see the illustration). To complete the booklet project, a student writes two statements about each category on its corresponding page; then he illustrates the pages.

• This center idea reinforces students' reading skills and their understanding of community services. On different colored sentence strips, write a sentence about a community service in three different colors as shown below. Make each sentence self-checking by writing the numeral 1 on the back of each strip of the first sentence, the numeral 2 on the back of each strip of the second sentence, and so forth until each sentence has been programmed. Mix the strips together and place them in a large folder labeled "Community Mix-Up!" To complete the activity, the student reads each strip, arranges groups of three strips into sentences, and flips the strips to check her answers.

| The public works department | provides communities | with clean water. |

| Schools | are places | where people learn about things. |

| Police officers and firefighters | work | to keep us safe. |

| A community park | is a place | for people to have fun. |

Serve It Up!

*Serve up a hearty helping of goods and services
with this made-to-order lesson.*

Skill: Distinguishing between goods and services

Estimated Lesson Time: 35 minutes

Teacher Preparation:
Duplicate page 85 for each student.

Materials:
1 copy of page 85 for each student
1 rubber ball (or beanbag)
scissors
glue

Background Information:
In a community, people use goods and services
each day. *Goods* are items that people make or
grow, such as clothing and corn. *Services* are jobs
that you pay someone else to do for you, such as
car repairs and checkups with a doctor.

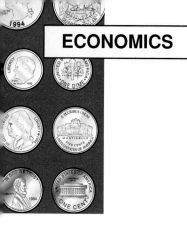

Introducing The Lesson:

Toss the rubber ball to a student. After the child catches the ball, have him name something bought from a store, such as bubble gum or shoes. Then have the student toss the ball back to you. Record the youngster's idea on the chalkboard under the heading "Store Items" (see the sample list). Continue in this manner until half of the students have named a store item. Then follow the same procedure with the other half of students, having each of them name an occupation, such as teaching or repairing cars. Record students' ideas on the chalkboard under the heading "Occupations" (see the sample list). Then explain that each word on the chalkboard is either a good or a service.

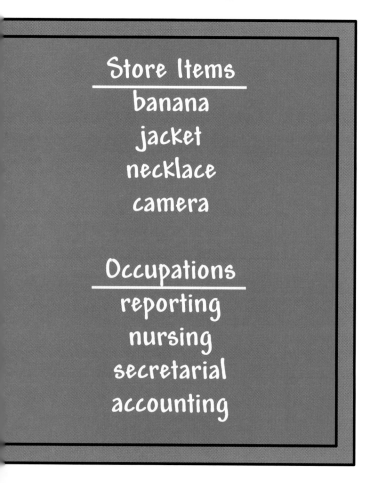

Store Items
banana
jacket
necklace
camera

Occupations
reporting
nursing
secretarial
accounting

Steps:

1. Share with students the Background Information on page 83.

2. Direct students to read the words on the chalkboard. Have them determine which column of words includes goods and which includes services. Change the "Store Items" heading to "Goods" and the "Occupations" heading to "Services." Then ask students how each good or service helps people in a community.

3. Distribute scissors, glue, and a copy of page 85 to each student. Ask a volunteer to read aloud the directions at the top of the page. Have each student complete the reproducible independently.

4. Challenge students to complete the Bonus Box activity.

Name _____

Distinguishing between goods and services

Serve It Up!

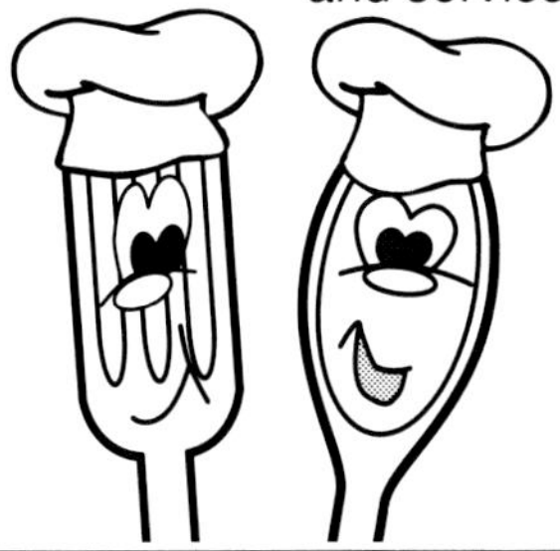

Read the words on the boxes.
Cut out each box and glue it on the matching menu page.
On each box, write your answer to the question.

Gourmet Goods	Scrumptious Services
Who provides each good?	What type of service does each worker provide?

Bonus Box: On the back of this sheet, write three more goods and three more services.

©1999 The Education Center, Inc. • *Lifesaver Lessons*® • TEC515 • Key p. 95

postal worker

car

doctor

lifeguard

books

fruit

farmer

shoes

How To Extend The Lesson:

• Show students several goods that they use daily, such as a toothbrush, a comb, food, a pencil, and a book. Have youngsters orally share why each good is important to them.

• Brainstorm with students a list of services provided in your school (teaching, cleaning, cooking). Record students' ideas on the chalkboard. Under your students' direction, write the name of each person who does the job next to the service. Then have each student write a thank-you note to a different school helper. Direct her to include in the note the goods and services the employee provides and how the worker helps the school community.

• Put goods and services in the spotlight with this art activity. Divide the class into small groups. Have each group think of a place in which both goods and services are provided, such as a grocery store or a department store. Then give each group a length of bulletin-board paper. Have the group write goods and services associated with its place in the middle of the paper. Direct the group to draw a box around the lists and write the name of the location underneath it. Next have the group draw pictures around the box of the goods and services to create an eye-catching border. Display the completed projects around your classroom, and encourage youngsters to check out the many goods and services provided in the different locations.

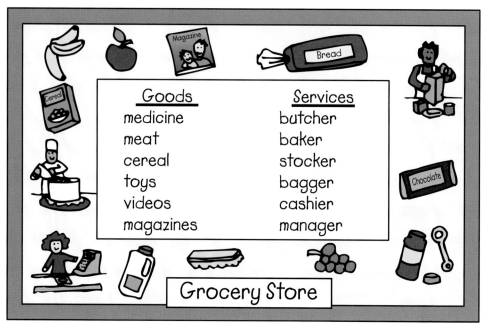

Monkeying Around With Labor

Swing into a study of specialization and division of labor with this "ap-peel-ing" lesson!

Skill: Applying an understanding of specialization and division of labor

Estimated Lesson Time: 40 minutes

Teacher Preparation:
Duplicate page 89 onto white construction paper for each student, plus one extra.

Materials:
1 white construction-paper copy of page 89 for each student, plus one extra
1 set of crayons for each group
1 pair of scissors for each group
glue for each group

Background Information:
In communities people share their learning and work to complete big jobs. People do different jobs to save time. *Division of labor* is the breakdown of a whole job into parts. It is a faster way to make goods. *Specialization* means a person focuses on a certain part of a job.

Introducing The Lesson:

Draw an outline of a car on the chalkboard (see the example below). As students name different parts of a car, label each part on the car's outline. Ask students how they think the parts are put together to make a car. Explain that cars are built in factories using division of labor and specialization.

Steps:

1. Share with students the Background Information on page 87. Explain to students that they will use division of labor and specialization to create decorated gift boxes.

2. Divide the class into groups of four students. Give each group four construction-paper copies of page 89, scissors, crayons, and glue. Have a student volunteer read aloud the directions on a copy of page 89. Ask youngsters to name the tasks necessary to complete the gift box (decorating, cutting, folding, gluing).

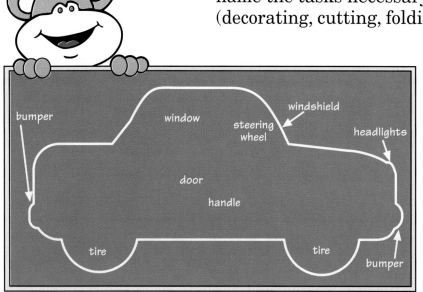

3. Using the extra copy of page 89, demonstrate for students how to fold and glue a gift box.

4. Assign one student in each group a specialized task (decorating, cutting, folding, gluing) to be completed for each box. Explain that making these job assignments is an example of division of labor. Remind students to work on each box quickly and neatly. Then direct each group to use the patterns and materials to assemble four gift boxes.

5. After students have finished their projects, have each youngster tell about his experience. Discuss with students how division of labor and specializing in a particular task helped to finish the project faster or better.

Applying an understanding of specialization and division of labor

Directions:
1. Decorate each pattern as desired.
2. Cut out the box and lid patterns.
3. Fold the patterns on the dotted lines.
4. Glue the tabs to the inside of the box and lid patterns.

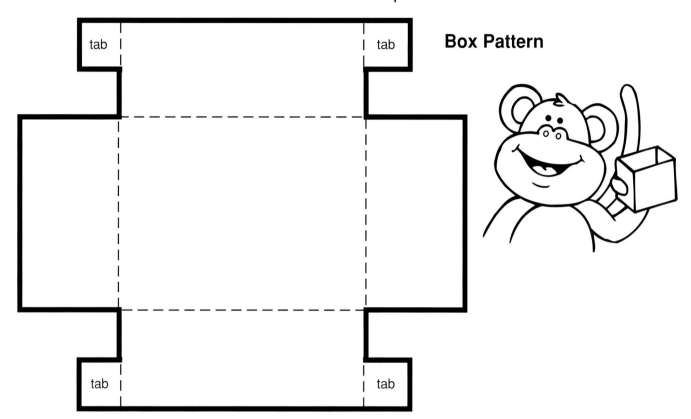

Box Pattern

Lid Pattern

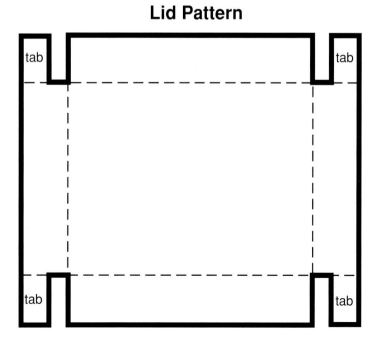

89

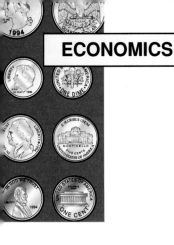

How To Extend The Lesson:

• Have youngsters practice division of labor by creating candy trucks. Divide your class into teams of four students. Tell students that each group will be completing four candy trucks. To create a candy truck, one student breaks a large graham cracker into four smaller pieces. Then he uses a

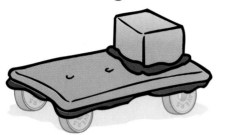

knife to spread a thick layer of frosting on one piece. The next child attaches four Life-savers® candies to the frosting on the cracker for the wheels (see the illustration). The third student frosts the bottom of a caramel cube and attaches it to the top of the graham cracker for a cab. The last child carefully places the edible vehicle in a resealable plastic bag. Have the groups repeat the procedure until each child has a candy truck.

• Help an overworked hen by applying an understanding of specialization! Read aloud *The Little Red Hen* by Paul Galdone (Houghton Mifflin Company, 1985). Tell students that because the hen did everything to make the flour, the least her friends could do is make the cake! After sharing the story, direct youngsters to list the tasks involved in preparing the cake (gathering sticks, building a fire, mixing a cake). Then ask students which job would best suit each animal (cat, dog, mouse). Have students share their choices and reasons for them. If desired, delve deeper into specialization by having pairs of students write an advertisement for a job mentioned in the story.

I need a doctor to give me drugs to sleep during surgery. (*anesthesiologist*)

I need to have my heart checked. (*cardiologist*)

I am having trouble with my skin. (*dermatologist*)

I need to have my blood checked. (*hematologist*)

I am having trouble with my nervous system. (*neurologist*)

Something is wrong with my eyes. (*ophthalmologist*)

My baby is sick. (*pediatrician*)

I need a doctor to read my X ray. (*radiologist*)

• Illustrate the concept of specialization by taking a closer look at the medical profession. In advance, create a list of specialist-related clues such as, "I am having trouble with my heart. Which doctor should I see?" Post a list of medical specialists that correspond with the clues. Then read each clue about doctors and enlist students' help in matching it to the corresponding specialist. Encourage each youngster to find out more about a medical specialty that interests her.

Applying an understanding of specialization and division of labor

Producer Or Consumer?

Students discover information about consumers and producers with this hands-on activity.

Skill: Understanding that a producer is a consumer

Estimated Lesson Time: 30 minutes

Teacher Preparation:
Duplicate page 93 onto light-colored construction paper for each student.

Materials:
4 chairs
1 construction-paper copy of page 93 for each student
1 brad for each student
scissors
crayons
writing paper

Background Information:
A *producer* is a person who makes goods or provides a service. A taxi driver, a baker, and a teacher are all producers. A *consumer* is a person who uses goods or services. A person who pays for a taxi ride or buys bread is a consumer. When a producer spends the money he earns, he is a consumer too. For example, a taxi driver (a producer) is a consumer when he pays for fuel. The money goes from consumer to producer and back again.

Introducing The Lesson:

Arrange four chairs to represent a car (see the illustration below). Then sit in the driver's seat and tell students to imagine that you are a taxi driver. Pretend to start the engine and ask if anyone needs a ride. Select two volunteers to sit in the backseat and ask them where they need to go. After a few moments of driving, apply the brakes and tell the passengers the amount of their fare. Have students pretend to pay you before they return to their seats. Next, as you drive off, announce that your taxi needs fuel and you are driving to a gas station. Ask for a volunteer to fill your taxi's tank. Once the tank is full, ask her how much you owe and pretend to pay her. Then have her return to her seat.

Steps:

1. Explain to students that you have just acted as a producer and a consumer. Then share the Background Information on page 91 with students. Ask students for other examples of a person who is both a producer and a consumer.

2. Distribute a copy of page 93 and a brad to each student. Have students color and cut out the patterns. Instruct students to assemble the wheel by inserting the brad first through the wheel and then through each hole of the strips.

3. Ask a student volunteer to read aloud the first example on the wheel. Have students determine if the baker in this situation is a producer or a consumer. Confirm the correct response and have each student rotate her corresponding strip to align behind the example. Continue in this manner until all examples have been read and identified.

4. Finally, on a sheet of writing paper, have each student list three situations when a doctor is a producer (for example: *gives shots, gives physical examinations, and checks eyes*). Then have the student list five situations when a doctor is a consumer (for example: *buys office supplies, pays power bills, and buys equipment*).

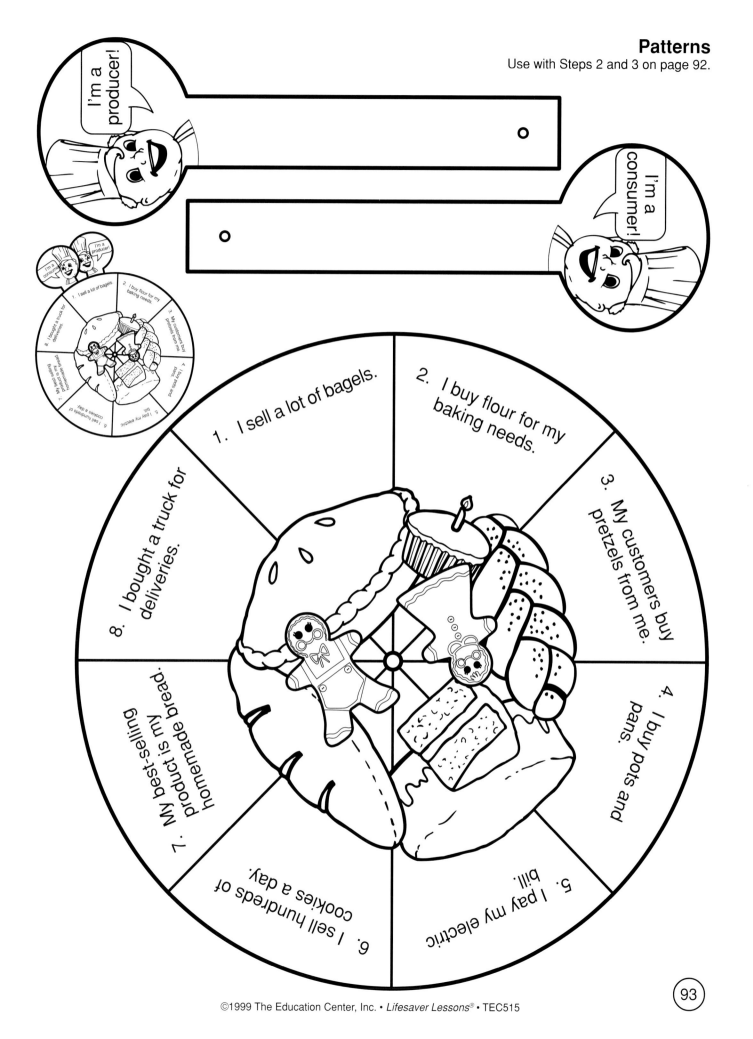

I'm a producer!

I'm a consumer!

1. I sell a lot of bagels.

2. I buy flour for my baking needs.

3. My customers buy pretzels from me.

4. I buy pots and pans.

5. I pay my electric bill.

6. I sell hundreds of cookies a day.

7. My best-selling product is my homemade bread.

8. I bought a truck for deliveries.

ECONOMICS

How To Extend The Lesson:

- Have each student construct a collage of consumers and producers. For each student, cut a large, construction-paper *C* and *P* or, if desired, have students make their own. Provide students with discarded magazines and instruct each student to glue pictures of consumers on the *C* and pictures of producers on the *P*. Then have each student attach a self-adhesive star on each producer that is also a consumer.

- Explore the travels of a dollar bill in the book *The Go-Around Dollar* by Barbara Johnston Adams (Simon & Schuster Books For Young Readers, 1992). After reading the book aloud, enlist students' help in creating a chart that shows the exchanges the dollar encounters. Label the people involved in the exchanges as consumers or producers.

- This center game reinforces memory practice *and* student understanding of consumers and producers. Label index cards as shown below; then place the cards in a center. To play the game, two students shuffle the cards and place them facedown. Then the first player turns over two cards. If the two cards have corresponding information, the player keeps the cards and takes another turn. If the cards do not match, the player turns the two cards facedown and the other player takes a turn. The game is over when all cards have been taken. The player with the most cards wins!

mechanic repairs cars	mechanic producer		dog groomer bathes dogs	dog groomer producer
mechanic buys tools	mechanic consumer		dog groomer buys dog shampoo	dog groomer consumer
teacher teaches children	teacher producer		chef cooks for people	chef producer
teacher buys supplies	teacher consumer		chef pays for food deliveries	chef consumer

Understanding that a producer is a consumer

Answer Keys

Page 9

(Answers may vary.)
1. The police officer keeps people a safe distance from the fire.
2. The police officer keeps people out of the way so the firefighters can do their job.
3. The firefighters don't have to take time to apply first aid to victims because the EMTs will do it.
4. The police officer keeps people out of the way so the EMTs can do their job.
5. The firefighters bring injured people out of the building so the EMTs can work in safety.

Bonus Box: (Answers may vary.) Citizens can help by staying out of the way of the rescuers.

Page 17

(Answers may vary.)
1. Keep your dog on a leash.
2. Ride your bicycle on the right-hand side of the road.
3. Bag yard clippings. Do not burn trash within the city limits.
4. Do not leave open barrels or containers in your yard.
5. Do not let poison oak or poison ivy grow in your yard.
6. Put litter in its proper container.
7. Wear a helmet when in-line skating.

Page 29

Everglades

These marshlands, found in Florida, have plains of grass and trees.

You'll find a variety of wildlife here including alligators, cougars, manatees, and many birds.

Statue of Liberty

It's a long way to the top! From its feet to the tip of its torch, this sculpture is over 150 feet high.

What a popular place! Each year about two million people visit this statue of a robed woman.

Grand Canyon

Carved by the Colorado River, this hole in the ground is over one mile deep in places.

At sunset the red and brown layers in this canyon's walls are a beautiful sight.

Mount Rushmore

This huge sculpture of four U.S. presidents is found in the Black Hills of South Dakota.

These four faces are George Washington, Thomas Jefferson, Theodore Roosevelt, and Abraham Lincoln.

Page 37

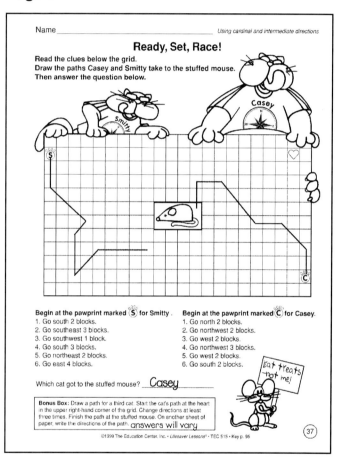

Bonus Box: Answers will vary.

Page 41

1. D3
2. E1
3. B4
4. C1
5. E4
6. C3
7. A4
8. B5
9. video (Answers may vary.)
10. A1

Bonus Box: fuel at D5 or repairs at E2

Page 45

1. symbols
2. 4
3. apples
4. 4
5. apples
6. corn, peanuts
7. peanuts
8. cotton, peanuts, apples
9. peanuts
10. corn; Corn is the product that is grown the least.

Bonus Box: (Answers will vary.) cotton picker, peanut butter producer, apple juice producer

Page 50
Bird's-Eye View

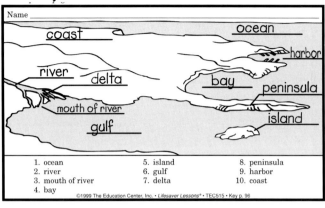

Page 49

1. B
2. H
3. C
4. J
5. A
6. F
7. G
8. E
9. D
10. I

1. harbor
2. island
3. gulf

Bonus Box: (Answers will vary.)
1. A peninsula has water on three sides and an island is completely surrounded by water.
2. A gulf is larger than a bay.

Page 53

1. Atlantic Ocean
2. Indian Ocean
3. Antarctica
4. Asia
5. South America

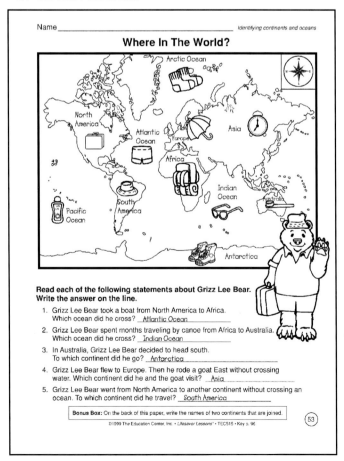

Bonus Box: North America and South America **or** Europe and Asia **or** Africa and Asia